FundaMENTAL W.E.A.L.T.H. Principles

FundaMENTAL W.E.A.L.T.H. Principles

DEVELOPING A MINDSET FOR FINANCIAL SUCCESS

Clyde Anderson

Vice President, Publisher: Tim Moore
Associate Publisher and Director of Marketing: Amy Neidlinger
Operations Specialist: Jodi Kemper
Cover Designer: Alan Clements
Managing Editor: Kristy Hart
Project Editor: Elaine Wiley
Copy Editor: Apostrophe Editing Services
Proofreader: Anne Goebel
Indexer: Angie Martin
Senior Compositor: Gloria Schurick
Manufacturing Buyer: Dan Uhrig

For information about buying this title in bulk quantities, or for special sales
opportunities (which may include electronic versions; custom cover designs;
and content particular to your business, training goals, marketing focus,
or branding interests), please contact our corporate sales department at
corpsales@pearsoned.com or (800) 382-3419.

For government sales inquiries, please contact
governmentsales@pearsoned.com.

For questions about sales outside the U.S., please contact
international@pearsoned.com.

Printed in the United States of America

First Printing November 2013

ISBN-10: 0-13-349206-0
ISBN-13: 978-0-13-349206-4

Pearson Education LTD.
Pearson Education Australia PTY, Limited.
Pearson Education Singapore, Pte. Ltd.
Pearson Education Asia, Ltd.
Pearson Education Canada, Ltd.
Pearson Educación de Mexico, S.A. de C.V.
Pearson Education—Japan
Pearson Education Malaysia, Pte. Ltd.

Library of Congress Control Number: 2013949129

This book is dedicated to my "Why," my wife,
Jan Anderson. Thank you for putting up with me and being
an audience of one whenever I need you.
You are the best wife a man could ask for.
Thanks for being my blessing.

Contents

Acknowledgments

They say the journey of a thousand miles begins with one step, so I want to thank not only the people that watched, helped, and guided me as I took the steps to make this journey a success, but those that also carried me when I felt like I couldn't walk any more. No one walks alone on the journey of life, and nothing great that has ever been accomplished was done without the support of a great team. Where do you start to thank those that served as my crutches, confidants, council and companions? I guess at the beginning....

Thanks to all who listened to me share the W.E.A.L.T.H. Concept with them and shared their feedback. Thanks for the therapeutic conversations that took place across the country as we began the "W.E.A.L.T.H. Movement" that was created to get people to change their minds and ultimately their lives by increasing streams of income and managing their resources. Thanks to Steven "Bo" Beaudoin who ensured I had a positive mindset and has served as my wise council. Tenisha Taylor Bell, what can I say, Sis, but thanks for seeing something in me and being willing to take a chance on me by putting me in front of millions on a weekly basis. You are definitely a game changer. This book and its pages will be seen as "thanks" to the tens of thousands of you who have helped make my life what is today. Much of what I have learned over the years came as the result of sharing, hearing, reading, being transparent, and helping you to go from where you are to where you want to be. A huge source of inspiration originates from being a father to my three wonderful little ladies who I call my princesses, Taylor, Cayden, and Mackenzie, all of whom, in their own ways, inspired me and, subconsciously contributed to the mindset that pushes me daily to be the best me possible and never say "I can't." A piece of each of them will be found here weaving in and out of the pages—thanks ladies! Thank you to my mother Gwendolyn who taught me humility, how to care for others, and to share my values, thoughts, and expressions with those who are in need by showing me how to understand their needs. You are the best mother in the entire world! I also have to thank Reverend Charles G. Adams who showed me what a true orator is and can be. Thanks to Dennis Kimbro, a wonderful man who changed my thought process completely and showed me what was possible. I continue to think and grow rich, and I owe much of that to you.

Thanks to all who helped to show me how to maneuver the streets of Detroit and how to be a man when my father was gone. It is through the teachings, encouragement, and support of so many that I have gained and grown. Through this book and my travels I will continue to spread a message of fundaMENTAL techniques that help people live the lives they envision and leave their comfort zone to reach their destination of freedom. I will continue to share the method to change minds and watch lives follow.

About the Author

Clyde Anderson is the author of the bestselling book *What Had Happened Was...* and a seasoned Finance Expert, lending his advice and valuable expertise to radio and television for more than 6 years and appearing on CNN more than 400 times. With more than 12 years invested in the personal finance sector, Clyde has guided thousands of families from coast to coast to financial independence. He has also consulted with hundreds of national corporations and trained dozens of industry professionals on the principles of economic empowerment using his practical approach to encourage and inspire.

Selected as a CNN "New Guard," which identifies and honors current and next generation newsmakers, Clyde is a nationally acclaimed speaker, commentator, consultant, coach, author, blogger, and trainer covering topics from the state of the housing market to blueprints for financial success. Clyde's ability to relate to "Middle America" has established consumer loyalty, respect from industry heavy weights, and a stream of noted accolades. Clyde has been featured in several national publications, television, and radio shows. Clyde's experience has not only taught him how to persevere, but how to plan and appreciate the value of a dollar. He is the premier authority on personal finances because he has lived through challenges and achieved success by "practicing what he preaches." He is an example of how to achieve financial empowerment and entrepreneurship through practical planning, innovation, and strong relationships.

Clyde currently lives in Atlanta with his wife and three daughters.

Introduction

Do you want to be wealthy? I don't know many people who would say no. But let me be clear; this isn't some get-rich-quick book that harnesses the secret to building wealth. Rather, it is a tool to help you develop a mindset that helps you focus your thoughts in the right direction to achieve the success you desire.

The reality is it's not about the money. You are here now, in this state of mind, at this stage of success or failure because of your thoughts. Previous thoughts and actions shaped your present financial life, whereas current thoughts and actions can shape your financial future. If life has been a challenge, chances are your mind is plagued by what I call negative or poor thoughts. These thoughts carry over into every aspect of your life leaving little room for dreams or growth, creating the right environment for doubt, fear, and complacency to sprout. You become stagnant waiting for things outside yourself to move you where you want to be instead of moving yourself.

It's hard to move when thoughts keep you bound by your past mistakes. This bondage is so strong it corrupts any chance for change. But all is not lost. There is hope. It doesn't help that the media is constantly telling you that things are rough, and the times are bad, but in reality they are prime for picking. The good news is that you have the power to transform and discipline your poor thoughts. You can reverse negative thinking that has become commonplace in your mind as well as the influence it has over your life. When the cycle of negative thoughts is broken, your life can begin to change. You can eliminate thoughts that bind you and replace them with positive, or W.E.A.L.T.H. thoughts, that allow images of freedom, determination, and pure will to position yourself for financial success!

It's the power of your mind, thoughts, and emotions that decide how your day, week, month, year, and eventually your life is going to manifest, along with the level of financial success you will attain. The first step is to believe that it's possible. Because you're reading this book, I would venture to say you do have a level of belief. Sure, it might need to be strengthened and reinforced, but don't fret. That's exactly what I'm going to help you do.

Before you start, I have to ask the question: Do you think you can achieve financial success? Until you answer this question truthfully, you can't proceed. If you don't believe you can, you've already lost. If a tennis player steps on the court thinking she can't outplay her opponent, she might as well pack up her racket and leave. If a boxer enters the ring feeling his opponent will out-box him, it's just a matter of time before he will be kissing the canvas. The power of suggestion can be dangerous if not applied correctly or in a positive manner toward what you want to see in your life, instead of attracting what you don't want to manifest.

Your thoughts have power because you give them power. Your thoughts govern your words and dictate your actions. As thoughts grow and become fixtures in your mind, they give birth to other thoughts that connect to each other, growing stronger by each passing moment. As you think, your thoughts are made active, which in turn directs your attitude and reflects your current state of mind. No wonder change in economic status and personal finances have so many people feeling helpless, hopeless, and doubtful.

Although many people are hurting and struggling financially, everyone is not. There are currently approximately 12 million millionaires in the world and approximately 4 million of those are in the United States. So you must ask yourself, why? Why hasn't everyone succumbed to the poor economic conditions that seem to effect so many? The answer is discipline of thought and the power to control poor thinking, emotions, and the actions that accompany them.

You've heard stories of people who pick themselves up, rising from poverty to go on to do amazing things and experience great wealth. It wasn't luck, but rather the ability to discipline their thoughts that helped them embrace life-changing opportunities. Because of their actions that were driven by their thoughts, they are now thriving in the face of adversity instead of allowing their thoughts to defeat them and allowing unfavorable circumstances to stand in the way of having financial success.

You have a decision to make. You can choose to pursue your goals and desires, and achieve the level of success you dream about, or simply lie down and surrender. You can choose to embrace change and fight to win or let your thoughts forfeit your chances for success. Will you stand in the midst of adversity? Can you censor your thoughts long enough to see opportunities on the other side? The decision is yours to make. Let today be the day you decide to play to win for a better tomorrow using *FundaMENTAL W.E.A.L.T.H. Principles.*

I refer to W.E.A.L.T.H. as the ability to first be wise enough to know *who* you are. This doesn't mean the vice president of this or the manager of that. It's not about what you do or your title, but who you were created to be, what's inside of you yearning to be released. What do you love to do and would do for free if you could. This refers to the person that you were designed to be and your purpose for being. You also have to be wise enough to know *where* you are currently because it's impossible to get to the destination that you desire without first knowing where your point of departure is.

Think about that directory in the mall that helps you locate the stores you are looking for. There is a small sticker with an arrow that says: You Are Here. If that sticker weren't there, you probably wouldn't know how to get to the store you're looking for. The same is true of your life. It's crucial to know where you are. Are their gaps in your finances that keep you at the place you don't want to be? Are you where you want to be? If not, I can help you get there. You'll need to *establish* exactly *where* you desire to be by setting W.E.A.L.T.H. goals that are Workable, Empowering, Asset Producing, Leverage-able, Time-Sensitive, and Harvestable. This goal-setting process can help you stay focused and on the path toward your financial success. The emphasis in this model is based on the *mental* aspect because you are the sum of your thoughts. Henry Ford used to say that whether you believe you can or believe you can't, you're right either way. That's the power of believing.

The next step is to determine your *why*. Why do you want to be better, do more, and have more? Why do you want to change your financial life? Your *why* is what motivates you. It's what pushes you in the sea of life and propels you further, even when your arms feel like limp noodles and your legs are dead weights. Your *why* will wake you up early and keep you up late at night working. The key with why is to remember that it must be bigger than a paycheck. If that is the only reason you are doing what you're doing, the passion will be missing, and the amount you're receiving soon won't be enough to compensate you for your discontent. You will explore your nonmonetary assets; those things you possess that go beyond the traditional sense of valued possessions (that is, just money). Anything that is tangible or intangible that can be owned or controlled to produce value, and that is held to have positive economic value, is considered an asset. It's crucial to identify these assets in these economic times because you might not have a lot of money, but if you can assess what you do have and value—things like your time, relationships, gifts and talents, dreams, ambition, and knowledge—you can use them to earn the money you desire. Simply stated, assets represent value of ownership that can be converted into cash. It's time to evaluate what assets you currently have and are utilizing or under-utilizing. Even if you don't have cash in abundance, you have other forms of currency that can be as valuable, if not more.

Maybe it's time to look at ways to create additional streams of income, and utilizing your assets might be just what you need to create that stream to help you reach your financial or W.E.A.L.T.H. goals as I refer to them.

The next step is *leverage*. You'll discover and use it to create a "plan of action" to move you from where you are to where you want to be. Have you ever heard of a professional sports team that begins playing a game without a plan? Have you ever heard of someone building a house without a blueprint? If they do, they are destined to fail. You must have a strategy, a plan of action, to accomplish those things you want to achieve. If you don't have a clear plan, vision, or mission for your financial life, you will lack direction, guidance, clarity, and ultimately finances.

Lastly, you'll have an opportunity to create a strategy to *execute* your plan, with excellence, to get the *harvest* that you envision. The *harvest* is the fruit of your labor; it's the manifestation of your *why*. To realize the harvest, you must execute, or rather gather, the crops that you have planted over time to realize the benefits in your life.

Now, if you're ready, here's how we're going to do it....

This book shows you how to incorporate W.E.A.L.T.H. into every aspect of your life and how to use FundaMENTAL W.E.A.L.T.H. Principles to seize opportunity and begin your journey toward financial change.

There are two outcomes from this book. You can either read it unengaged from beginning to end, taking mental notes of how FundaMENTAL W.E.A.L.T.H. Principles for your financial life could possibly be applied to your own life and dream about financial change, or you can fully participate by being prepared to take action at each phase.

I often tell my clients that if you can change your mind, you can change your life. There are no cookie-cutter results. What you put into this change is what you will gain: If you don't put forth effort to maximize the information contained within these pages, you cannot reap the benefits of real change, maybe only a temporary fix. You must be willing to adopt a new mindset, yield new results, and improve the quality of your life.

FundaMENTAL W.E.A.L.T.H. Principles is a 14-chapter book broken into two sections. Both sections can help you explore the concept of discipline of thought, which is the ability to possess self-discipline to control your thoughts to achieve your desired results, to help you become a better money manager, and to achieve financial success for your life.

This book will explore the concept of W.E.A.L.T.H. using the acronymn "Wisdom to Establish Assets & Leverage The Harvest." This concept will be used to help you connect to the real you that has desires and is passionate about setting and achieving your goals. But because it's impossible to set realistic goals without having a *why*, which serves as your motivation to continue to press forward in the face of adversity, you will have an opportunity to *identify* and *define* your *why* that will motivate you towards your success. You will also *identify* and *define* the current non-monetary assets you possess that, if used properly, will help you achieve your goals. I often say if I had no money but still had non-monetary assets, I could and would use them to amass the currency I desire. You will also be provided a process that, if followed, will help you discipline your thoughts so random thoughts don't talk you out of reaching your destination or prevent you from achieving your goals. I will introduce a process that will help you become the master of your thoughts so that you won't be derailed in your pursuit of creating your W.E.A.L.T.H. You will learn how to leverage each of these components to realize your harvest which is the manifestation of your dreams, desires, goals, and resources.

FundaMENTAL W.E.A.L.T.H. Principles will introduce you to key concepts, including specific steps, tips, methods, or activities that evoke new perspective and allow information to further resonate on a deeper level through practical life application. These supportive objectives can enable you to interact with the book, develop a new mindset, and retain the material. What's the use of reading something that you can't immediately apply to your life?

At the end of the book, you create a financial success plan based on the information provided in the book. The financial success plan helps you become a better financial manager as well as helps you apply the lessons of disciplined thoughts to make better financial decisions. This is not theory; this is application in action. It's time to change your mind to change your life. Are you up for the challenge to make that shift a reality?

1

My Story

After serving as a financial analyst on CNN and other outlets for more than 7 years, I began to get the feeling that there was something more that I had to do after having conversations with many individuals who were struggling in their financial lives. When I say financial lives, I'm referring to the comprehensive concept and presence of money in, throughout, and over every aspect of their financial lives. To put it bluntly, most were broke and working to make ends meet, basically living paycheck-to-paycheck, or had a small (I use the term loosely) savings. I saw myself in each of these individuals and realized that if I hadn't been thrust into the role that I was at 23, I might be right there with them trying to figure it all out, still making the costly mistakes that set me back, adding years to my sentence of financial ignorance.

I can remember the phone ringing as my mother and I sat in our modest two-bedroom apartment in Detroit about a block away from 8 Mile Road, the street that Eminem made famous in his biopic film by the same name. I could tell from the surprised look on my mother's face the news wasn't good. Tears began to run down her face. It definitely wasn't good. My father had died. He lived in Chicago, and at the age of 32, had suffered a severe brain aneurysm and had slipped into a coma. One day later he was gone. My father's passing changed my outlook on life. To understand the impact, let me rewind just a little.

I was born in Milwaukee, Wisconsin. Yes, black people do live in Wisconsin. I was the first and only child. My early years were very pleasant. My mother was the youngest of ten and I was the last grandbaby. I was what you might call spoiled. I can remember having a plethora of toys. Other kids always wanted to come over to play with my drum set, my new action figures, or my remote control cars. I don't remember asking for much, but just remember having the things. This would become a regular occurrence in my life.

My parents married at 22. I was born when they were 23. They divorced not long after I was born. My mom and I moved in with her parents. They lived in a two-story duplex. My grandparents lived upstairs and a few cousins lived below. I developed a close relationship with my Grandmother, whose name was Ruby, and with my Grandfather Bennie. They were two beautiful old people in love and had been married for 50-plus years by the time I came along. They were special to me because they made me laugh and smile, showed me what true love was, and would give me whatever I asked for.

I can still remember my Grandfather stretching his cane toward me to grab my legs and pull me toward him. My Grandfather became ill, and before I knew it, he was gone. My Grandmother's heart gave out about 9 months later. The doctors said it wasn't a heart attack, but rather it just stopped beating. Many people believed that this was the result of losing the only love she knew. This was devastating to our family, but earth-shattering to my mother, who cared for them both and was the baby of the family. At 28, she had lost both her parents and felt lost herself. Two months later, my oldest uncle Bennie Jr. suffered a stroke and died also. My mother needed a change. She had to make a move to have a fresh start, so she decided to move us to Detroit, where she already had a brother and sister who both had families there. We packed and moved quickly. I can remember one of my going-away gifts was a T-shirt that read "Pray for me, I live in Detroit."

Welcome to Detroit

We settled into our one-bedroom apartment, which would be our home for about a year until our two-bedroom unit would be available. The community seemed nice enough and I was still around family. I was enrolled in a school by the name of Vandenburg Elementary that was located across the expressway that was about a 20-minute walk from my home. It was a better school, from the research my mother had done than the ones in the district we lived in. It was in my mother's sister Doris's district, so we used her address to enroll me. The plan was for me to walk to school in the morning and then go over to my aunt and uncle's home a few blocks from the school until my mother was able to pick me up after work. I don't really remember what my mother actually did at that time, but I know it was sales-related. It seems as though she always did something in sales. We didn't talk much about work, probably because it was the last thing she wanted to talk about after a long day. To be honest, it wasn't what I was interested in discussing either. I was just elated to see her.

I Lost It Before I Got It

Not long after my father died, I began to hear my mother on the phone in the evenings saying things like, "So what happened to the money? Will he get any? Shouldn't that go to Clyde?" Intrigued by what she was talking about, I began to listen more. From what I could hear, it seemed my father was entitled to some land not far from Memphis, Tennessee, that should have gone to his child, me. Instead, one of his sisters decided that it didn't belong to me, so she kept the part that would have been mine. My mother was furious. It all seemed so confusing to me. She explained it to me, in the way my mother always would, as if I were a little adult, that my aunt had taken what was supposed to be mine. Not sure of how that really affected me, it still made me sad since I had learned that you didn't take anything that wasn't yours. I never received any part of that land, which I later found out was worth several hundred thousand dollars.

I guess this was my first bad money experience, which was totally confusing because I always thought family was there to help you, support you, and make you feel better. Now I was learning that one of my family members had taken something from me that was worth money. "Why would she do something like that?" I thought. It's just money. Right?

What I Learned

This experience showed me that money had power. It obviously had the power to divide families and make people exhibit behaviors they may not if money weren't involved. At the early age of 8, I was now witnessing the ugly side of this thing called money. I resented my aunt for doing this because it seemed so wrong. Little did I know that things like this happened more often than not. It was a lesson in money and life. Maybe it was good I didn't get the money because, at the time, my money behavior which was passed down from my mother supported spending until there was none left.

It wasn't about being rich or wealthy for me. I saw large homes on television, expensive cars going down the street, but I never put that together to mean other people were rich. It just meant they were able to get what they wanted. I lived in an apartment while my friends lived in houses. I never thought about it being not as good as the way others lived, but rather that this is just how we chose to live. Did my mother want to purchase a home for us? Maybe. I'm not sure. We didn't discuss that. We just lived. That was home.

What Is Money for Anyway?

I've heard many people say they didn't realize they were poor growing up because they were shielded or sheltered from the harsh reality of not having enough money. My first tainted view of money was that it was something made to spend. This wasn't from a lack of mentality, but rather consumer training. My mother bought everything I wanted. She made sure I had nice stuff—toys, clothes, and everything else. When I got them, it made me feel good and made her happy to spoil me. She taught me early on to respond to the question that people would often ask, "Are you spoiled, Clyde?" to which I would respond that I was fortunate, not spoiled. I did feel complete because I got what I wanted and didn't have to work hard to get it. I just asked for it. I did the minimum required. I think this same mentality followed me into adulthood until I was slapped with the harsh reality that good things comes to those who work hard to make their vision a reality and execute their plan.

I think I might have been 5 when I was given money by my uncles every time I visited them. They just gave me a dollar here and maybe a two-dollar bill there. On a great day, I'd get a five. No one told me what to do with the money. I had seen my mother and others use the money to buy the things they wanted or needed. At 5, there weren't many things I needed that weren't already provided by my mother or others, so, of course, I began to use the money to purchase things I wanted like candy, toys, and that sort of thing. (I was beginning with no plan or direction. This never ends well.) Unbeknown to me, I was creating a money mindset that was not going to be conducive to building wealth of any sort. As a matter of fact, it was the complete opposite. It was a path to use all that I had to get what I wanted.

Sure, you might say I was just a kid and that I should have fun and use the money to get things I wanted. But I still could have done that and also saved maybe 20 percent for my rainy-day fund or future fund. Think about it. If I would have been educated about the power of compound interest and just saved some of the money I was given from the time I was 5 until now, even in a low interest-bearing account, I would have had a substantial amount and a foundation to begin on. Instead, I got a mouthful of cavities from too much candy that helped build wealth for some dentist whose name I don't even remember.

As I got older, that "easy come, easy go" mindset would prove to be the prevailing thought process that would govern my life. If I had money and wanted something, I would buy it. Or if I wanted something and didn't have the money at the time, I would find a way to get the money to just consume that thing. It's sad when you think about it. I was living to consume. My only strategy was to get, to have, and figure out the details along the way. My perception of money was that it was a tool to consume and nothing more.

I Thought I Was Rich

By the time I was 23, I had an income of about 200K annually. This was more money than most people I knew were making. I was a 100 percent commission mortgage banker in a small suburb of Orlando called Maitland, Florida. This is where I learned the art of sales, developed a heart to help others get from where they were to where they wanted to be, and learned that making a lot of money doesn't make you immune to the issues that those with less have. Because it's not what you make but how much you keep.

These lessons would prove to be instrumental to my development. At the time, I felt that I had enough money to spend. Trips to Aruba, long weekends at the beach, boats, nice cars, clothes, and all the exotic handbags my wife could carry became my reality. I was armed with a total disregard for managing money and a desire to have those things that I wasn't exposed to. That was my driver. Although I thought I was different, separated from those with less money, I possessed the same mindset. To my surprise, it was a poverty mindset that would keep me broke no matter how much money I made.

One day I was sitting around the house in Florida, bored. I began to think about some of the clients that I had been assisting who had large credit limits but marginal credit.

This was the mid-90s when as long as you had a decent credit score, a pulse, and could fog a mirror, you could get loans, credit cards, or anything else you wanted to borrow pretty easy. At the time, I had no credit cards. Everything I wanted I just paid for with cash. I figured I had nothing to lose, so I hopped on the computer and applied for a shiny new credit card online. Why not, I thought, what did I have to lose? I didn't realize that I actually had a lot to lose. I was applying for credit just because I could. I had no plan of action and was about to do something really dumb. In what seemed like seconds, I was approved for a new credit card and, to my surprise, this new card came with a $20,000 limit. I was elated with my new tool, one I really shouldn't have had.

My first mistake was getting a card I didn't need, nor one I was prepared for. My second mistake was not paying attention to the interest rate. When the card came in the mail, I noticed it was one of the newer mini credit cards that could fit on my key chain. Cute, I thought. But it was a wolf in sheep's clothing, one that I had no clue how to tame, as well as the 12 percent interest rate that came with it.

I still didn't realize the power I truly had, and what I could have done with it only if I knew how to use it appropriately. I charged it to the point where I had so much debt that I couldn't pay it off entirely in 1 month. The interest was building rapidly. I could have used it to build my credit, help with emergencies. I could have even used it to start a business. Instead, I used it foolishly and often. It became hard to pinpoint exactly what I had purchased by the time I had maxed out the card because I had invested in many everyday things like food, groceries, clothes, and other things that made me feel better. I used this card until the magnetic strip was fading off the back. As I continued to consume many small things with the card, I lost sight of how much I was actually spending at any period in time.

Without the physical reminder of bills or lack of bills in my wallet, I thought my supply was endless. It takes a long time to spend 20 grand is what I thought. But I was wrong. In truth, when I thought I had only $250 on small items in any given month, I actually had spent triple that, and simply not remembered because there was no accountability.

My monthly minimum payment on the card was $1,200. I can remember making the payment with little to no effort when the money was coming in rapidly, which really wasn't helping me, because that monster called interest, that can either work for you or against you, was definitely not on my side.

Wake Up Call

As the industry shifted, and mortgage rates increased, the money began to slow, and I began to wonder how I would make the monthly payment that at one time seemed like a piece of cake. This piece of cake now became a nasty mountain of old cake I had to climb, untrained and with no gear. I was determined to get the balance paid off, but after months of low or no income and struggling to make the payments, the balance went into collections. I vowed that this would never happen again.

This would be the beginning of my change, or what I like to call my financial awakening. My eyes were opened to what money was really about. I could make the money, but if I didn't manage the money, I would lose it fast. If

I were going to ever have more than I had, I would have to do things differently. I had to separate my wants from my needs and create a plan that would help me accumulate what I desired. I had achieved a level of financial success but wasn't prepared for it, so I lost it. I lost the opportunity to start building a substantial savings. Even worse, I had missed obtaining the security and financial independence that I now believe to be the freedom that people who possess wealth know as their reality.

I'd always wanted to be a great entrepreneur and break free from the confines of corporate America. Yet, I was thinking, "Yeah right, like that's going to happen."

You see, I was canceling the positive words or thoughts out with negative thinking. Although I didn't verbalize my fear of failure, one that had a Kung Fu grip on the progression of my life, I thought it. Therefore, it was so. I was destined to remain just where I was, waiting for something amazing to happen, waiting for that email that would change my life, the phone call that would help me step out of the door, or the contract that would give me permission to take a leap of faith. I know it sounds crazy, but that was my reality or the reality I had convinced myself to live daily.

My affirmation was...

> I have the ability to create wealth in abundance; I
> am a wealth creator.

I repeated this over 20 times a day. You might believe in affirmations and you might not. I didn't for years, but when I began to fill my subconscious with thoughts of success instead of thinking about what I didn't want to attract to my life, things began to become clearer. Any time I had a negative thought, which I had learned from experience was the beginning of more negative thoughts, I would soon become consumed with negative thoughts that usually kept me stuck and not able to move forward to accomplish the things that needed to be done. I was in desperate need of mentors whom I could identify with, ones who had overcome adversity and were living a purposeful life void of the lack that I was beginning to feel had become a permanent fixture in my life.

Section I

Your W.E.A.L.T.H. Mindset

2

All About You

The majority of your world is stifled with stress, even when things are going well. High unemployment, negative news on the television, fear of financial lack, recessions, the economic outlook and rising prices threaten you with additional stress and anxiety as you watch your retirement savings and overall financial future slip into jeopardy. The reality is that money is often on the minds of most of us. In fact, money and work are two of the top sources of stress for almost 75 percent of the population, according to a Psychological Society study.

Your conscious mind is a remarkable thing, but there's a whole other level of awareness that, when tapped, can greatly expand your abilities, and can allow you to achieve your goals in life. Follow these principles to learn how to access your subconscious mind. The more you learn about your mind and your thoughts the more you can enhance your life.

What Is the Subconscious Anyway?

The subconscious is the part of your consciousness that is not currently in your focal awareness. What made you throw that candy bar into your grocery cart as you stood in the checkout line? Underneath the layers of your critical thought, and the functions of your conscious or alert mind, lies a powerful awareness called the subconscious mind. Because there is a limit to the information that can be held in conscious focal awareness, a storehouse of your knowledge and prior experience is needed, and that is the subconscious. Your subconscious loves to do work while your body performs other tasks that are easy. Think about it. How many good ideas have you had while driving, in the shower, or sitting idle? When you are relaxed, yet slightly distracted, your mind is often at its best.

My own mindset was changed by focusing my subconscious on a certain issue. I started to see new angles and opportunities that I've never seen before.

The subconscious doesn't judge, create, or work without you telling it what to do, think, or repeat. The subconscious believes whatever you tell it to believe. Is it okay to have that candy bar, or is that a no-no right now because of a diet? You can use different methods to develop your subconscious mind. Listening to your intuition or gut feelings, making predictions, and answering yes-or-no questions are a few techniques. These help to open the subconscious parts of your mind to you.

You must trust your subconscious, speak directly to it, and believe in its capability to completely change your life. You are the master of your world, thoughts, actions, emotions, and responses. Be careful what's playing in the background of your life, whether it's a television, radio, or others talking. This awareness is one way to protect your subconscious because your mind can absorb ideas that you do not necessarily need.

Pay attention to what's happening around you, but refrain from getting caught up in doom-and-gloom hype that can lead to high levels of anxiety and bad decision making. Have you identified your personal, social money behaviors, messages, and images that shape the way you have viewed money in the past, as well as your current views? You have an opportunity to determine how you really feel about money and to explore why money is important to you. Avoid the tendency to overreact or to become passive. Remain calm and stay focused to identify your financial thoughts and make a plan. Take stock of your financial situation and what causes your poor thoughts.

THOUGHT QUESTION

Where does a positive money mentality come from, and what does it look like in your life?

How You Perceive Money

Have you ever thought about the way you perceive money? You might have grown up thinking money is hard to get, maybe hearing someone say, "Do you think money grows on trees?" It might have become for you this elusive commodity that slips through your fingers and doesn't want to be captured. In reality, it's waiting for you to get it, control it, tell it what to do, put it to work, and bring it the company it desires—because money loves to multiply.

When you are honest with yourself, you can admit that you might envy people who are millionaires—the way they live their lives, the things they own, or the way they enjoy life. All this might seem unattainable in your life. Or you tell yourself that it's impossible for someone like you to get there, so you settle for mediocre instead of what you really should be striving for, which is greatness and financial security. Like it or not, money is important.

People approach the concept of money in many ways and with varied types of behaviors. The first type of people are those who see that the world has insufficient money for everyone. These people think that money is meant for the rich who take it all. People with this mindset usually choose a mediocre life.

The second type is those people who see that the world has too much money. It's sufficient for everyone, and anybody can be wealthy. These people are people with a strong vision in life. They know they want to achieve big in life! I'm not saying that money brings happiness, but it will certainly make your bad times a little easier to deal with.

The New Normal

Whatever it is that you might be thinking, or might have thought in the past, it's now time to toss out the old way of thinking and prepare your thought process to achieve financial success in what I like to call The New Normal. What's The New Normal? Well, a shift has occurred in the world that has caused the economy to change. We've experienced multiple recessions that have caused many people to lose things they worked hard for: jobs, homes, savings, or the perception of security that kept them feeling comfortable. Although many people are waiting for things to blow over and go back to the way they used to be, the reality is that they won't now, nor will they ever. You must adjust your vision, skill set, thought process, and mindset to do something different to achieve the financial success you desire.

Can You Really Reverse Negative Thoughts?

Now that you've recognized that negative/poor thoughts are affecting your financial life, the question is how can you reverse these thoughts? How can you change the money mindset that you've developed and that's keeping you bound? How can you pick up the pieces and see past the "right now" to focus on what you believe to be possible? You must first create affirmation statements to help renew your mind and block negative thoughts. As you will recall, mine was, "I have the ability to create wealth in abundance; I am a wealth creator."

Begin by putting your statement everywhere you'll see it often...on the bathroom mirror, in the car, in your day planner, and at any other place where you look at least twice a day.

W.E.A.L.T.H. Affirmations

Here are some possible affirmation statements:

- My financial abundance overflows today.

- The presence of joy in my heart releases an abundance of good into my life.

- I was destined to be prosperous. I have abundance to share and spare.

- I fill my mind with the idea of abundance, and abundance manifests in all of my affairs.

- I release all feelings of lack and limitation.

- Today is rich with opportunities and I open my heart to receive them.

- Money flows freely and abundantly into my life.

- Wonderful things happen to me for I live with an attitude of gratitude.

- I always have more money coming in than going out.

- I allow myself to have more than I ever dreamed possible.

- I am abundantly provided for as I follow my path.

- I know my value; I honor my worth.

- All the money I spend enriches society and comes back to me multiplied.

- I am open to receive.

- My money is a source of good for myself and others.

- I am financially independent and free.

Just having the affirmation and seeing it daily isn't enough. You must meditate on it each time you're faced with a circumstance that will send your thoughts to that toxic place.

Nasty Negativity

Negativity often overwhelms you. It's no surprise, based on the images and messages that you digest on a daily basis. You might feel obligated to eat the negativity that is being served, but afterward you feel disgust that you allowed all those negative thoughts of lack and defeat to get inside you. You can't believe you ate the whole thing—one negative thought at a time—and now you're so full of negativity that you can barely move.

Negative thoughts don't just happen; they are there for a reason, and you need to follow the origin of the thought to discover why. The goal is to discover why you're thinking a particular thought and where it came from. Embedded in each negative thought is an important lesson you must learn, and the sooner you learn it, the better off you will be. This doesn't mean that after you do understand where it came from the negative thought will never appear again. However, you must practice the process of identifying the thought's origin and replacing it to make this process a habit that you practice and use as needed. You must develop a permanent strategy that eliminates these negative thoughts from your mind. Each negative thought contains the seeds of its own destruction. If you listen to its message, you're destined to fail. Problems remain problems until you discover their solution. It doesn't matter if a problem surfaces a million times; after you know the solution, the problem loses it power because you know how to deal with it. If you have a problem making and managing money, you must get to the root of the problem and know exactly why this has become a problem. Is it that you have never learned or that you don't have enough discipline? Or maybe it's lack of opportunity. Whatever it is, you must understand the origin of your thoughts. If you haven't learned, it's time to get educated—and let the fact that you hadn't learned it go because this is not time for dwelling on what didn't happen. If your problem is discipline, you can use the following approach to begin building the willpower to reach your financial mandate to be a better manager and identify what you can do to increase your income.

MIND CHANGER

You can replace negative thoughts about money with healthy, safe thoughts about abundance and believe that you can have what you desire.

Do you often have negative thoughts going through your mind? This usually occurs because you haven't formulated a plan of action to defeat them. Your mind lacks the security it seeks to be at peace when you aren't at peace because of your negative financial thoughts.

These debilitating thoughts can become powerful as they circle the tracks in your mind. The more you focus on these thoughts, the more momentum you give them, and the stronger they become, making it harder to stop these endless cycles of thoughts. But, if you replace these with positive thoughts, you can steer yourself upward and away from negative thoughts and results. It's similar to a basketball team that has been on a winning streak and eliminating every opponent in their path. It builds confidence and intimidates the competition. The more games the team wins, the stronger it becomes. The momentum and success rate is due to the energy the players use to reign in their minds and stay away from negative thoughts.

No Plan

For years I found myself unable to defeat the thoughts of never climbing out of my financial hole, not making what I needed to rebuild or make ends meet for that fact. It was 2009 and the writing was on the wall. The mortgage industry had shifted; I had begun creating affordable housing programs with the Atlanta Development Authority for the then Atlanta Mayor Shirley Franklin. We were using bonds to create a pool of funds to provide assistance to people who wanted to move into the city. After successfully leveraging more than $50 million in bonds, I began to get the feeling that it was time for me to go. I knew it was time to venture out on my own and take a leap of faith. This was one of the hardest things I've ever had to do, and I often tell people it was like jumping off a building and not seeing the net below or knowing how to fly. I decided to take the leap and create my own consulting firm to do some of the housing work I had already been doing. Several people told me they wanted to work with me, and I felt confident that it was the right time. As soon as I did take that leap and walked away, I was on my own, ready to take over the world. But there was one thing I had forgotten. I didn't have what I now call a financial success plan. In my mind I had a plan, but it really wasn't a formal, written plan. I hadn't listed my financial goals and milestones. I hadn't solidified contracts. Nor did I have a strategy to get the contracts to ensure that income would be flowing into the business. Here I was now, in a world in which it was literally sink or swim, without a plan.

It wasn't long before I had used all my savings and had taken a huge chunk out of my retirement account because it was taking longer than I thought it would to get up and running. If I would have had a plan, I could have reduced the time and heartache caused by venturing out into the world of business without it. When I developed my plan, things began to shift. It took the guessing out of business—well, at least the part I could control. I created a plan for my personal finances as well. I knew exactly what I needed to make my household run efficiently, what I needed to save, what to re-invest, and where any gaps or surpluses were. Because I took the guesswork out, this was one less thing I had to worry or even think about. I could focus on what was important because it's much harder to manage having nothing than it is to have something to manage. My plan was helping to give me the resources to manage. I had learned to be disciplined enough to create a strategy and stick to it. Now my life was about to change.

Why Discipline?

Discipline is used in modeling character and for teaching self-control and acceptable behavior, such as teaching children to wash their hands before meals. Washing hands before meals is a particular pattern of behavior, and children are disciplined to adopt that pattern. Are you adopting new patterns or even controlling the ones you have? Do you have the discipline to manage your money and not make purchases that don't help you reach your goals? You must create a pattern that becomes second nature. You must become the master of your thoughts and use them as your motivation instead of letting them be a deterrent.

The phrase "to discipline" often carries a negative connotation. This is because of the need to maintain order—that is, ensuring instructions are carried out. Order is often regulated through punishment. But discipline can provide many benefits when it's the key to achieving what you want in life. Discipline, in that context, is used as the assertion of willpower over base desires and is usually understood to be synonymous with self-control. Because self-control places you in the driver seat, it's desirable and up to you to make sure you have what discipline you need to reach your thought destination. It's time to tell yourself what you should be thinking, or, in other words, produce and direct the show rather than being a spectator of your own mind.

The Process of Disciplining Thoughts

This simple idea was first given to me while I was at an entrepreneurship conference in Atlanta where I live. A popular magazine was hosting the conference at a downtown hotel. As I sat at the bar in the plush hotel, I began speaking with a gentleman sitting next to me. I'm always interested in meeting new people and potentially making a new connection or learning something new.

"How are you enjoying the conference?" I asked.

"Well it's my 20th time at one of these and I still enjoy it," he replied. He went on to explain that he and the owner of the publication that created the conference had grown up in business together, so he was always there to support. I learned that we had something in common because we were both from where I was raised, Detroit, Michigan. His name was Bill, and he was a high-ranking executive with a large car manufacturer in Michigan as well as a frequent

White House visitor and consultant. In essence, he was a Power Broker, meaning he was a go-to guy who was very connected and could make things happen. As we continued talking, the conversation shifted as it normally does at this point to finances and the economy. It's always interesting for me to hear different perspectives and potentially learn something new. Bill began by asking me a question that would change my life.

He turned and looked at me and said, "Did you know that at the Harvard School of Divinity they focus on discipline of thought before doctrine?"

I was intrigued. If this were true, then Harvard realized that no matter what you're planting, you must first prepare the soil. Or, in this case, it's the mind's soil that must be prepared to receive, retain, and apply the information that could potentially change lives. I don't think Bill realized what that simple statement did for me. It literally turned the concept of financial literacy upside down for me. I was eager to see how I could integrate this fascinating concept into my teachings. It didn't take me long at all. It was almost like I could hear the word "wealth" being whispered in my ear. But as fast as I heard the word, I also heard it as the phrase: "Wisdom to Establish Assets & Leverage The Harvest." It happened just like that. Excited, I sat down with a pen and a pad and the concept was born.

Preparing Your Mind

By thinking debilitating thoughts constantly and dwelling on them, you are providing such thoughts the power they need to expand. The more you feed your negative thoughts and ideas, the more they grow, and the more power they gain. The same is also true for your positive thoughts. Therefore, your goal should be to increase the positive thoughts and decrease or eliminate your negative ones. Sounds simple when you see it in writing, but if you've ever tried to change, you know it's one of the hardest things for most people to achieve. Although it's hard, it's not impossible. With some intentional action you can take control of your thoughts and ultimately your financial life.

Here is a list and explanation of the defensive steps needed to take control and discipline your thoughts, to defeat them, and take a step closer to financial success:

1. *Identify it*—You must identify your competition before you can even think about achieving success.

2. *Face it*—Take a deep breath and become aware of what you are dealing with, and set a course of action of how to confront each trigger that causes the negative or poor thoughts.

3. *Record it*—In sports, a game log keeps track of the wins, losses, dates the games were played, as well as player statistics.

4. *Replace it*—Replace each tired or foul thought with something positive. Affirmations and positive thoughts enable you to begin the process of changing your mind to focus on thoughts that can benefit your life.

5. *Practice it*—Persistence pays and repetition builds habits.

To make this process work, each step must be applied to each thought. Defense wins games, and positive thoughts are the genesis to achieving the financial success you seek. You must be willing to submit to the defensive process if you truly want to change your life.

THOUGHT QUESTION

What do you think about most as it relates to your personal finances? How have these thoughts affected your life?

Brain Invasion

When something is invaded it has been taken over and occupied, and the control has been turned over to a more powerful force. My question for you is, are you ready to hand over your thoughts and your mind to the powerful force called positivity? You are living in unprecedented times when the act of thinking and the thoughts you create have become more important than ever. You can't solely base your thoughts on what you see. Instead you must see beyond what's in front of you. It's "time out" for living on default or autopilot. The model, or lack of model, that was in place in the past for financial success is not what it used to be. Many opportunities are now masked as adversities that you see as obstacles instead of stepping stones, mainly because your mind doesn't see them as such. You are one of many visual people; you have a mental photo album. The snapshots in your mind often associate the pictures you see now with those negative realities from your past. Without new positive realities to replace those old images, you find yourself clinging to the examples of your past. You find yourself following the same blueprint or roadmap that was created during another time in history and is no longer effective.

MIND CHANGER

You become what you think about most.

THOUGHT TIP

Another positive thinking technique is to visualize your future success. There are some people who think about their failure, even before starting a project, but that should be avoided at all cost. When you have planned what you want to achieve, visualize how you would like to see yourself.

3

Identify Poor Financial Thoughts

Critical thinking is a logical process that considers all the facts on any situation, not dwelling on a one-sided perspective, or hopes and fears. To work, it has to call on the part of the mind that looks at things rationally and logically. Unfortunately, if you have any financial anxiety locked into your emotions when the feared situations occur, this activates the part of your mind that deals with guesses, perceptions, and the willingness to swallow ideas whole. It makes logical thought somewhat impossible.

Negative thoughts often come so quickly and automatically that you are unaware of them. You start to feel bad, but you don't notice the thoughts that are causing you to feel that way. To counter these thoughts and feel better, you first need to become aware of them when they happen. You have to catch yourself in the act of negative self-talk, especially when you deal with new situations, or situations that have always been difficult for you, such as money management or wealth creation.

Types of Self-Talk

These negative messages are the enemy to a positive, abundant, and successful life. But amid the many and constant thoughts that occur in your mind, learning to identify and recognize those that are harmful messages can be tricky. Their well-disguised messages slip into your mind, often unnoticed. Sometimes they communicate in words, other times with images, and sometimes an impression is enough to ensure your support of their agenda. There are several varieties of self-talk and they each have different roles. You have lived with these various characters for so long that you often are not even aware of them. They are experts at disguising their messages so that they appear as rational, logical, or responsible concerns. You are often aware of their warnings, alarms, or condemnations. Yet you don't always recognize that their input is negative, misleading, or totally false.

Four Basic Types of Thought Characters

Following are four basic thought characters. These character descriptions can enable you to identify your own negative thoughts more easily. You must determine if the thoughts that seem troublesome sound like the Backseat Driver, the Defeated, the Financial Fret, or the Superhero.

The Backseat Driver: Feeds on Low Self-Esteem

The Backseat Driver is constantly analyzing and judging you. He emphasizes your weaknesses, flaws, shortcomings, and past errors. He compares you to others by highlighting their best qualities and contrasting them with your weaknesses. It's like he's telling you that you should have gone left when you went right or you wouldn't have gotten into that accident. The same is true with your finances. He downplays your financial accomplishments by pointing out how you could have done better. You would have had more money if only you had done something else. You were lucky to get what you did because you're not smart enough or that everyone can do that; it's not special. He might even blame you for what others do. (If you had reminded your friend about picking up your check, he might not have forgotten.) And he expects perfection. A Backseat Driver can never be satisfied no matter how good of a driver you are. No matter how great of an effort you make, you will never please the critic. His role is to find fault and he does his job well.

The Defeated: Promotes Depression

The Defeated tells you that you are incapable of making your way in the world. He points out your powerlessness to change issues that you are facing. How could you possibly manage your financial life when everything you do is turning out bad, in a world where the rich get richer and the poor continue to suffer? You'll never make a difference. He also likes to convince you that you are responsible for other people's feelings. He puts you in a Catch-22 and then points out the hopelessness of your situation. He also convinces you that there is something wrong with you, which is why you haven't achieved financial success. He doesn't stop there because he continues to make you believe you deserve to be exactly where you currently are, and that's all you need or are going to get. He is your reminder that you have failed, when in reality you have succeeded at some point or another, even if in a small way. He says you have no right to expect anything better than what you get because you're unworthy; you don't deserve to win.

The Financial Fret: Promotes Financial Anxiety

The Financial Fret always anticipates the worst and envisions images of destruction and financial ruin. He creates an image of always losing and having bad luck with your financial life. This character conjures images of lack, hardship, and "what if" hypothetical scenarios of financial failure starring you as the main character. This character uses your insecurities and anxious feelings to legitimize the negative thoughts. If you decide to make an investment that you've planned and are prepared to make, he will worry you about all the reasons you shouldn't and what might go wrong. So you backtrack and second-guess your decision. Then he worries you about a new set of issues resulting from the delay of backing up or not going through with the investment. Because you don't know what might happen in the future, you can't discard the entire picture. In the midst of negative news on television and stories of failure all around you, this character will keep you not just confined to your home, but also hiding under the bed until everything blows over, scared to make a move.

The Superhero: Promotes Stress and Burnout

The Superhero is a relentless master. He is intolerant of the notion that you are human. That most humans aren't perfect is just an excuse to him. He is never satisfied with anything you do or achieve. He constantly reminds you that you could have done better, saved more, invested more, or maybe less. You should have known the idea wasn't going to work. You should always perform at a superstar level, never get tired, be sick, or feel any pain. He will analyze everything you do, every decision, every interaction, and inform you of how you could have done better. He convinces you that your worth as a person is based on the greatness of your financial achievements and how hard you work. He doesn't care what it takes to get it done, or who loses in the process as long as it's done. He always expects more than is humanly possible and then scolds you for missing the mark. Basically, he tells you that you will never be good enough.

Why We Have Them

Poor thoughts and self-talk are an accumulation of self-limiting messages that you have become in the habit of saying to yourself. Breaking this destructive habit is possible, though it takes some time and consistent effort. If you have been talking to yourself for a long time, it will take repetition and practice to learn more constructive and helpful ways of thinking. Your competition is your Poor Thoughts. Whenever a negative thought enters your mind, take the time to first acknowledge it, and then deal with it. To identify a particular thought, you must step outside of yourself to study your thoughts and recognize where the problem exists, where the thought originated, and understand what trigger brought it on. You must see the thought for what it is and survey the complete picture to identify the thought, define, describe, and analyze the thought to accurately evaluate it. This will allow you to classify the thought and proceed.

Are You Ready to Take Control?

Are you willing to do what it takes to experience true freedom and change your Financial Thoughts? The freedom I speak of is the freedom you can experience if you have control of your finances. Freedom to explore and not be required to work for someone else unless you choose to, going and coming as you please, and just enjoying your life. The reason you haven't experienced this true freedom is not because you don't want freedom, but because it is not what you are used to, or not what you've seen, or not what you've experienced. Freedom resides outside of your comfort zone. Freedom means sacrifice, hard work, and facing the unknown. This is true in your work as well as your thoughts.

Whenever a negative thought enters your mind, immediately step outside of yourself and take time to identify the source. Pinpoint where the problem exists and the triggers that caused your toxic thoughts. This can help you understand where your negativity begins and enables you to recognize it before it escalates and wreaks havoc in your mind.

Point out the random thoughts that you have that have no direction:

- Are you having thoughts that are moving you closer or further away from your goals?
- When you are having random thoughts that are not connected to your purpose, how do you feel?
- Are the random thoughts fact or speculation?
- How do you guard your thoughts?
- Can you identify triggers that spark negative thoughts about your personal finances?

THOUGHT QUESTION

Are the words you use conducive to the change you desire to see?

MIND CHANGER

As you think, your thoughts become active, which in turn directs your attitude and reflects your current state of mind.

4

Face the Thoughts

Running or burying your head in the sand to hide from the little monsters in your mind that tell you all sorts of awful things will just allow them to compound and will eventually cause more damage than good. If you don't face these poor thoughts, you will never challenge them and overcome them. You have to acknowledge your feelings. If you're thinking about it, it already has power. You must address the root of the problem that caused the thought and stand up to it.

The reality is that 80 percent of everyone's thoughts contain some sort of negative content, so having these negative thoughts is a normal part of life. The secret is to recognize them when they occur and then control your response to the thoughts when you recognize them.

You Give Up Your Power

When you refuse to face and experience your feelings, you give up your power to control them. It is you who have given them power. To stop this, you need to be willing to accept that feelings are a part of life. When you deny your feelings, you diminish your life experience and limit your awareness of your personal experience. Your life is only one-half lived because you cannot avoid your feelings. Only your conscious knowledge of these thoughts as they exist inside you—creating chaos, whether you are aware of it or not—can free you. You must be willing to experience those feelings that you have tried to avoid by control, submission, or plain out avoidance.

Throughout each day, while you go about your routine, you consume stimuli, which often bring negative thoughts as you attempt to solve problems. The difficulty isn't that you have negative thoughts. The problem comes when you believe your thoughts are true and let them consume your mind.

The thoughts in your mind work together to create stories that are often false, but your beautiful and powerful mind makes them sound believable. The problem is that you buy into these stories and take ownership. You don't step back to get a better perspective. You don't ask yourself necessary questions about your thoughts, such as, is this thought true? Is this thought important? Is this thought helpful? These simple questions help to put the thought into perspective and determine its validity.

Label your thoughts. Instead of saying, "I'm terrible with money," say, "I'm having the thought that I'm terrible with money." Instead of saying, "I'm never going to have any money," say "I'm having the thought that I'm never going to have any money." The difference might seem subtle, but it can help you gain the perspective that you are not your thoughts.

Thank your mind. If you're having anxious thoughts, such as, "I hope I'll be able to get out of this debt...I hope I don't lose my job..." say, "Thank you, Backseat Driver, for attempting to keep me safe, but there's nothing that you need to do right now. I've got it under control." Make notes to yourself and let your Backseat Driver know when it can take a break.

You must learn to talk to you yourself like a friend instead of an enemy. When you start to feel anxious, upset, or sad, take it as a signal to pay attention to what you are thinking about.

The reality is that most negative self-talk is false, irrational, and self-defeating. It makes sense that the first thing you want to do is question what is happening and not just let your bad feelings marinate in your mind. You must ask yourself what are you saying to yourself that is making you feel upset? Do you really want to do this to yourself?

Breathe Deeply

Negative self-talk often creeps in and happens so automatically that it can be hard to figure out exactly what you are saying to yourself. It is important to find a way to calm yourself so that you can slow your mind and thoughts, and detect what negative messages you are using. A quick way to relax is to take many deep abdominal breaths.

Every thought you have goes through the same process when it's developed. It's similar to creating plays for a sports team to execute. Some work, but others do not. You must explore them before you discard them. The goal is to respond to the landscape and alter the plan as needed.

You must do more than just develop thoughts. You need to execute at a level that moves you toward your goal. You must be the master of your thoughts and work to eliminate self-defeating talk that ensures you lose before you even begin to play.

Respond to Negatives with Positives

Write down a positive and nurturing statement that counteracts the negative self-talk. Make it in the first person. For example: "I learn from my financial mistakes whenever I make them."

Meditation is the best way to control your thoughts. Meditation involves the art of concentration and quieting the mind. In meditation, you not only control your thoughts but you also bring qualities of inner peace and oneness to the forefront. Tap into the calming power of your heart and use it as an alternative force to take the place of the negative mind. Meditate on positive thoughts and words of affirmation daily. (There are a number of sources where you can learn to meditate or refine what you already know.) If necessary, meditate as often as needed, day and night, to keep negative thoughts from taking over your mind.

When you spend all your time and energy avoiding, denying, or suppressing your feelings, you cannot focus your energy and awareness on your goals and dreams or enjoy your life. If you don't face your feelings, they will continue to push you until you can face them. Thinking happy thoughts to cover your feelings only delays the inevitable. Keep putting this energy into a container; sooner or later it's going to explode, no matter how much you affirm or visualize it staying contained.

Visualization is wonderfully effective when used to create your own experience. Just like it sounds, it means clearly seeing all aspects of a situation, decision, or dilemma you face. For example, when you experience fear, self-doubt, or anxiety about a situation or a thought, visualize yourself in that situation or of having that thought. Imagine that you are being, doing, and acting in your own best interests as you envision yourself. Most important, believe that the outcome will be favorable. Then you are better prepared to do and act in your life.

Take a deep breath and prepare to confront each trigger that causes negative thoughts. Running away or burying negative thoughts will cause them to compound and fester in your mind. After you identify what causes your negative thoughts, it's better to face them head on. Challenging negative thoughts when you first recognize them can help diffuse their power to expand into every area of your life.

Only by having the courage and wisdom to experience your feelings and know who you are, where you are, where you want to go, why you want to go there—keeping aware of the assets you have to get you there—can you become an empowered person who is insightful, purposeful, organized, and free.

When you decide to face and experience your feelings, know yourself and your life, you are free to choose your response to each situation. With no call to action, the self-talk will fall silent and you will instead hear your own inner guidance. And that message is always life enhancing:

- Focus on the thought that you are having and determine if it is a complete thought or a half-thought that has no merit.

- Is this a reoccurring thought?

- What is the worst thing that can happen if this thought became reality?

- Is the thought negative or positive?

- What is the lesson you can learn from this thought?

- Visualize your life without ever having these thoughts.

THOUGHT QUESTION

What reoccurring thought do you have that keeps you from pressing forward?

MIND CHANGER

Realize that feeling stuck can be temporary if you take the steps to change.

5

Record the Thoughts

D o you ever wonder why you think the thoughts you do? Do you have negative thoughts that occur again and again that you just can't silence? Keeping a journal for an extended period of time lets you learn the truth about yourself and your thoughts: how your motivation triggers change, based on what's happening. How many opportunities have you lost because your thoughts or perceived outcomes had no merit? It's important to document your thoughts until you become familiar with them and know how to manage and control them.

Journaling is a powerful process. People have been placing their thoughts, memories, fears, hopes, frustrations, joys, challenges, plans, sorrows, and victories in writing for many years. You can use this process to determine how your past experiences or current desires affect your thought processes and your life. By writing down your thoughts, you can reflect on them at a later time and see them in a clear, objective light, which can be therapeutic. Also, you can determine the areas where improvement can occur from this process.

You can use your journal to reference and track the important events in your life. Journaling allows you to reflect on the decisions that you've made and to examine where the deficiencies might be, but also to record your successes to inspire and uplift you. Your notes might serve as your blueprint or guide to where you need to go. Journaling has been proven to offer increased cognitive skills and serve as one of the most cost-effective forms of therapy—you can use your journal to write down positive thoughts or affirmations, as well as to help counter-attack specific situations that conjure negative thoughts. Making a record of your experiences and thoughts is an act of transforming your thoughts into legible words to provide a potential sense of relief and joy. Journaling provides significant benefits to your psychological well-being and thought process. Several researchers have shown that people who journal report having significantly less stress and have an overall better thought process. In addition, individuals also report that journaling can increase your emotional well-being and a better day-to-day mood.

Create Your Journal

Write down the negative thoughts or inner dialogues that led you to feel anxious, sad, or depressed. The act of writing down the negative self-talk helps you to see it as separate from yourself and makes clear exactly what the thoughts are. It might take some practice to do this and you will need to separate your thoughts from the feelings that come as a result of them. You can attempt writing down the feeling first, for example, "I'm anxious," and then the thought that led to it: "I will never have enough money." Remember self-talk involves thoughts, not feelings.

When you write in your journal, don't focus on just following the trail to find the cause of your negative thoughts. Also document your positive wealth thoughts. It might take a while for you to notice the effect, but you'll soon see faster change in your financial life because you will tend to move toward what you focus on. This is a powerful way to focus on growth.

I recommend keeping two separate journals: one to record your daily thoughts and activities and the other to track figures and expenses. By tracking and documenting your thoughts, you can study and reflect at will. This also helps you to monitor your progress or lack thereof and to determine if you are improving. Ultimately, your journal can be a huge component to achieve the discipline, control, and change you seek. Seeing your progress in black and white helps you to carry on when your motivation is at rock-bottom, and sometimes the knowledge that you'll have to record your failures is enough to keep you on the straight-and-narrow.

Create tabs to your blank book or create different files to organize your thoughts to different types of situations, occurrences, comments, images, or words spoken.

Start with a basic reaction to the thought. What was it about? How did it make you feel? What did it make you want to do? Were you inspired or discouraged?

Add concrete facts of what the situation is rather than how your mind perceives all aspects of it.

Add personal details. What is going on in your life while you are having the thought? Have you had a negative experience that served as a trigger to open the gate to negative/poor thoughts?

Track all your expenses, even if they are just a nickel. John D. Rockefeller kept a journal with every purchase he ever made since he was a kid. By doing the same, you can look back at your purchases for a week, month, or year and know exactly where your money went to eliminate stress and stay on top of your situation before it gets on top of you. Having such information can also help teach the FundaMENTAL Principles.

Record a daily record of poor thoughts. If you use it every day for a couple months, you will find yourself automatically countering your negative thoughts with positive self-talk. You will feel much better and more able to handle the stress in your life. Make copies of it and use it every day.

Write in your journal whenever you feel like it, and never get discouraged because you've let some days pass between entries. Only you can set the rules for your financial journal, and anything you choose to do in it is valid:

- Pour your thoughts onto the page for a head, heart, and hand experience about when you feel lost.

- Look for thought patterns and reoccurring or similar lost thoughts.

- Purge your mind of old thoughts and any thoughts that clog your mind and make you feel lost.

Go Deeper

Set aside a period of 10 minutes to write a journal entry every day. Even when you don't believe you've had any significant thoughts or have anything interesting to say. Just write something. Even if you are one of the busiest of people, you can find 10 minutes in the day. Set your alarm earlier, if you have to. It's worth the effort to write at least 150 words a day, which can take about 10 minutes. When you make journaling a habit, you'll find it much easier to manage your thought process and particularly the poor thoughts that have the potential to keep you confined.

Pick a poor thought you want to eliminate: Perhaps you can't stop thinking what might happen if you don't earn enough money to pay your power bill. For the next week, write down what you are doing each day to ensure that you do have that amount, but also how much you earned that day to move closer to achieving your goal. It'll take only a minute or two, and you'll see if you progress as the week goes on.

THOUGHT QUESTION

Do you remember exactly how you felt 5 years ago? If not, you might want to think about keeping a journal to document your past experiences and feelings.

MIND CHANGER

Documenting my experiences and feelings allows me to take myself out of the situation and see it from a new perspective.

6

Replace the Thoughts

Thought replacement is one of many ways you can manage your negative thoughts. This method is useful when you feel yourself sliding toward negativity again. Your awareness of your thoughts can give you a clue about any possible shift into a negative mindset and help you get ahead of it. All human beings have times when they are in a negative slump for a while. The goal with this awareness and replacement process isn't to completely prevent negative thoughts from ever entering your mind. That just isn't realistic. The idea is to improve your ability to reduce and manage the negativity in your mind. This can keep your brain from getting bogged down and keep you from becoming stagnant every time you are distressed about something.

You can use new positive thoughts and affirmations to set up a new plan in your mind. Through this process you can eliminate the thoughts that steer your mind down a path that leads to more negativity and lack of focus on your goal. You can use positive financial affirmations to develop a holistic, positive mindset toward money. Thus, positive self-affirmation allows you to develop a positive mindset toward every endeavor, personal as well as career or business.

As you acknowledge and release the negative thoughts about your finances, you can start introducing new thoughts in your mind. First, consider some of the positive changes or actions you are doing or can take. When you release a poor thought about your finances, say something new to yourself like, "I'm feeling more in control because I have cut down some of my expenses," or, "I'm finding methods to use my money in a smart way that causes it to grow instead of disappear." Use the positive information you are learning from your challenging situation to stay encouraged.

Counter Thoughts

Newton's Law of Motion states that every action has a reaction. The same is true with your thoughts. For every thought you have, there is a counter-thought, always a thought waiting to respond to each thought you have. The challenge comes if you don't realize that you can train or condition your mind to respond in a positive way. Instead you develop triggers in your mind, over time, which respond in a negative manner. It's a protection mechanism of sorts that has gone haywire and now has a mind of its own, and that can lead to negative thoughts.

Negative thoughts are the ones that destroy the healthy thoughts. When you're faced with situations and circumstances that breed unhealthy thoughts, instead of facing and disarming them, you unknowingly fuel them with the energy they need to grow by dwelling on them, contemplating them, running the worst-case scenarios through your mind until one of those might seem the only scenario. You can wallow and marinate in these negative thoughts, constantly revisiting them and letting them run amok in your head like rabid dogs.

Most of us don't think about the thoughts we're having or the thousands of choices and decisions we're making every day based on thoughts we don't even know we're having. So it's no surprise that your negative thoughts influence your decisions, actions, emotions, and finances in a negative manner. By allowing the negative thoughts to infiltrate your mind, they subsequently have a huge effect on your financial life. This is not a theory, but rather what I (and many others) have experienced. Your thoughts can be physically, emotionally, and financially dangerous because they are so powerful. You must harness and embrace this power to control your thought processes.

In my case, I was thinking that I wanted to be this great entrepreneur and break free from the confines of corporate America. But, at the same time, I was thinking, "Yeah right; like that's going to happen." I was canceling the positive words or thoughts out with negative thinking. Although I didn't verbalize my fear of failure, that fear nevertheless had a Kung Fu grip on the progression of my life. I thought it; therefore, it was so. I was destined to remain just where I was in middle management, waiting for something amazing to happen, waiting for that email that would change my life, the phone call that would help me step out of the door, or the contract that would give me permission to take a leap of faith. I know it sounds crazy when you think about it, but that was my reality or the reality I had convinced myself I lived in daily.

The Two Financial Thought Paths

Table 6-1 shows eight common negative thoughts along each thought path. These are thoughts or emotions that I consider to be negative or poor thoughts. Beside them are eight opposite, positive thoughts that I refer to as W.E.A.L.T.H. Thoughts.

Table 6-1 Negative and Positive Thoughts

Poor Trains of Thoughts	W.E.A.L.T.H. Trains of Thoughts
Lost	On Purpose
Fear/Anger	Faith/Joy
Lack	Abundance
Procrastination	Do It Now
Excuse	No Excuses
Pressure	Release
Ignorance	Knowledge
Blame	Responsibility

Replace each negative thought with positive thoughts and words of affirmation. Positive thoughts and affirmations allow you to begin the process of changing your mind so that you can focus on thoughts that can add value to your life. Use W.E.A.L.T.H. thoughts and affirmations to push poor thoughts out of your mind. Cleanse your mental palate with positive thoughts and start to develop a holistic, positive mindset toward finances.

When you identify the main concern driving the negative thoughts about your finances, which is a lack of control, when you do something that makes you feel more in control, you take the fuel out of your negative thoughts. You feel less threatened by the negative statements you hear in your mind because your emotions are calmed by your actions. "I'm never going to make it out of this money mess" has less power when you start getting results from your actions like a check from a project.

Write the poor thought on a piece of paper and shred it, ball it up, or burn it to watch your negative thought go up in smoke. Name your thoughts. Many times your thoughts are repetitive and involve the same thought. My thought frequently is, "I don't really know if I'll be able to do this." When thoughts come up along that story line, I can say, "Here's my 'I'm not able' story," and just let it go.

As you achieve more success, you build locomotive momentum that keeps you encouraged and moving forward. When you start to put better and more encouraging thoughts into your mind, they will begin to come more easily each day. Negative thoughts might still rear their ugly heads, but maybe not so frequently, or with as much muscle. The poor thoughts become easier to replace because your feelings are driven by more W.E.A.L.T.H. thoughts. Just as negative thoughts can build and feed on themselves, positive ones can do the same. This takes work and patience, but letting go and replacing the thoughts as they come can tame the raging stream of negativity:

- Why are you having this thought?

- By eliminating this thought, how might your life improve?

- Tell yourself that this thought has no place in your mind and must be eliminated.

- Think about what you have to be grateful for instead of what you are lacking.

Go Deeper

Write yourself an affirmation statement to help renew your mind and block negative thoughts from your mind. Put this statement everywhere you can and meditate on it each time you're faced with a circumstance that will send your thoughts to that negative toxic place.

THOUGHT QUESTION

Do you think more thoughts of lack or abundance?

MIND CHANGER

Realize that it's not about the money at all, but rather how you think about the money. You must overcome your current mindset to create one that will foster growth and change.

7

Practice Positive Thinking

Y ou must become a professional thinker; one who knows what it means to discipline your thoughts and use them to meet your needs and goals. You must learn to do it now. You can't stop until the process is ingrained and becomes a part of your everyday life. Think new or positive thoughts that help you succeed constantly and meditate on them daily, repeating the process over and over until it becomes a part of your subconscious and you see the changes in your thinking.

Persistence Pays and Repetition Builds Habits

Repeat the process of identifying poor thoughts, facing the triggers that cause them, replacing negative thoughts with positive affirmations while journaling your experiences, and you will eventually change your mindset. Don't stop until the process is ingrained and becomes a part of your everyday life. See a change in your thinking and see a change in your financial life.

You might not quite believe yourself at first because you are so accustomed to your negative thoughts guiding your decisions and life. If your thoughts are reasonable and encouraging, continue saying them to yourself, instead of anticipating disaster. Your more positive thoughts will pave the way for solutions you might have never considered before. By doing this, you can begin to convert your problems into opportunities.

Positive imagery can also influence your mind. If you know you respond to this, you should create a particular image with your positive thoughts to give them the weight they need to become permanent features in your mind. Perhaps a place you've visited, something you want to achieve, or an object that represents you being in control.

Practice this daily to begin to discipline your thoughts. When you allow the Poor Thoughts to creep in and violate your mind and run routes of disaster on your psyche, it's mostly because you don't believe you have the power to change your thoughts. In this case, you can often make yourself sick instead of making money. You dwell on the past because that is all you know. Besides what's going on right now, it's the only thing that is real to you. Your experiences are the sum result of things you've witnessed, heard, or learned. Sometimes your experiences have a way of staying with you, especially the negative. It's up to you to build the habit of positive thinking.

To Be Oppressed or Free, That's the Question

It might seem easier to allow negative thoughts to remain because you don't know the steps or are unwilling to put forth the work to eliminate these interferences that block the Financial Thoughts that assist you to win and achieve Financial Success. To make this process work, each step must be applied to each thought. Defense wins games, so you must be willing to submit to the process if you truly want to change your life.

I recently attended a boxing match that illustrated the fight you probably encounter daily in your mind. The underdog, who many had ruled out, was taking a beating unlike any that I had ever seen. He was pummeled by the powerful blows of the champion. The underdog was knocked down several times. His eyes were swollen shut, and it looked like it was over. I immediately equated this to what thoughts often do. They beat you up to the point that you feel like giving up. They make you feel like all possibility of winning is lost. You are knocked down by the events that seem to overcome you and strip any chance you have of succeeding. This is when it's decision time.

Making a Decision

You must decide whether you succumb or fight in the face of adversity and challenge. Because you are not prepared, it doesn't take much to knock you clean off your feet and cause you to lay flat on the canvas of life, motionless and still, waiting for someone to pick you up instead of doing it yourself.

The underdog had conditioned and prepared himself for this moment, something many of us neglect to do. After sitting in his corner and regaining his composure, the underdog came out swinging with a renewed sense of energy. I'm not sure what his corner man said to him in those brief moments, but whatever it was, it was just what he needed to realize the fight wasn't over. After the bell rang, he seemed to draw on a renewed sense of faith and energy to back it up. It wasn't long before the champion was down and out on the canvas with no hopes of getting up. The underdog had found a power deep down within himself that was the key element needed to turn his situation around to win the fight of his life. This is the power that all possess, but most choose not to tap into it.

This resembles the decision I was faced with. I had always thought I was a positive person, but when my life depended on it, I found myself making a decision to take the road most traveled and remain complacent. I was deciding that I couldn't do more; I couldn't be more. I was sabotaging my own destiny with thoughts that I had created, seen somewhere, or maybe even experienced in my past. These thoughts were becoming who I was only because I didn't know how to discipline my thoughts. That is, until I became my own corner man and talked myself out of that.

Tell Yourself the Right Words

A recent study highlighted in *Psychology Today* describes how speaking aloud helps you create two forms of memory. You remember the words both from reading them and from hearing them aloud.

Never say, "I can't." Just believe that you can and do your best. How will you know unless you push yourself? Constantly say things to yourself like, "I can," "I will," and "I believe in myself." Another aspect is to play around with words that make you happy and instill confidence in you. Make sure that the words you use evoke power and a sense of achievement.

W.E.A.L.T.H. Thoughts start with self-talk. Self-talk is the constant flow of unspoken thoughts that run through your head every day. These automatic thoughts can be positive or negative. Some of your self-talk comes from logic and reason. Other self-talk might come from misconceptions that you create because of lack of information. If the thoughts that run through your head are mostly negative, your outlook on life is more likely negative or poor. If your thoughts are mostly positive, you're likely a positive person or just practicing positive thinking.

Positive thinking is contagious.

When you are in the company of people who think positively, it spreads like a healthy virus, making you feel good about yourself. On the other hand, if you have even one friend who indulges in poor thinking, this will surely affect you in a negative way, spreading to you like a bad cold germ. So, your goal is to spend your valuable time with people who think and speak positively. Positive thinking is the key to success. By thinking in a positive way, you can maintain your focus and interest in your tasks and reach new heights.

The positive thinking that typically comes with being optimistic is a key to manage any stress you might encounter due to financial issues. If you tend to be negative, you can learn a lot from positive/W.E.A.L.T.H. thinking skills.

W.E.A.L.T.H. thinking means that you approach the financial unpleasantness in a more positive and productive way. You think the best is going to happen, not the worst.

As you get familiar with this process, you might find that it gets easier over time. There is no magic wand to take away negativity and problems in life, but you hold the key to the quality of your financial life, and negativity doesn't have to be in charge. You might not want to save money, but instead just spend. You must visualize yourself going through the motions of saving the first couple of weeks. Just start putting funds away a little at a time. Taking these baby steps will set you up for your saving program rapidly. Then after a few weeks, just go for it. Now that you have your emotions geared toward jogging, it should spur you into action. By allowing the emotional momentum to build, you can create motivation that will help you accomplish things that make you happier.

THOUGHT QUESTION

What are you telling yourself daily?

MIND CHANGER

Many of the thoughts you have on a daily basis are random thoughts which serve as triggers that prompt negative and anxious emotions, usually causing stress.

SECTION II

W.E.A.L.T.H.
Wisdom to Establish Assets & Leverage The Harvest

8

Defining Financial Success for Yourself

F inancial success looks different to everyone. To you it may be a large home, new Mercedes in the driveway, and ample money in the bank to do with as you please, when you please, and whenever you please. For some others it might be the peace of mind to know that the necessities are covered along with a few wants.

What Is Financial Success?

Envision, for a moment, yourself in your old age sitting and looking back over your life. What would make you say that you achieved financial success in your lifetime? When you think about the question, "What is financial success?" what is the first thing that comes to mind? Is it acquiring more material items, or as I call it, "stuff"? Maybe paying all your bills early, extensive travel, or eliminating the mountain of debt that's hanging over your head. Maybe you want to feel fulfilled, or feel that you have the freedom to do whatever you choose, or you may just want to consume more things. Usually the answers you supply when asked that question are superficial layers that need to be peeled back before you get to the core of defining this meaning of success for your life. It might take some time for you to get to your true realization. Financial success likely represents every good feeling that you want to experience to a greater degree. On an emotional level, money equates to a happier, freer, more meaningful life, but it's not the money alone that does it. Without purpose, it can be a hollow victory.

The reality is you can't live independently from your finances.

No matter what you do or where you go, finances are needed to carry you through. You can't look at creating a spending plan and then think about enjoying your life separately. You must fuse the two to ensure that you have the resources to live the life you desire. Not embracing this concept is one of the reasons many people experience a sense of depression when their sources of finances run low or become stagnant. Your financial life dictates how you run your household, take care of your family, and support your friends. It also sets the tone for your mindset and emotions. If your personal assets are not in order, it's more challenging to get ahead in other areas of your life. You constantly focus on what you don't have, causing your financial growth and maturity to become stagnant, putting the rest of your life on hold, never embracing the change that could ultimately improve your life and place you in the right direction for success.

Financial success looks different to everyone on this planet. No one has the perfect meaning of success although many try to accomplish the right look. If you want true happiness and long-term success, you must define what financial success means to you and have a vision of what success looks like in your own life. Think about it. Is it being self-sufficient, having multiple streams of income, a beautiful marriage and family, a great job, or maybe a business of your own?

Many see success as the accomplishment of an aim or purpose; therefore, financial success should be the accomplishment of a financial aim or purpose. In determining your own definition of financial success, think about what you are aiming for and what purpose you are fulfilling financially.

I've interviewed hundreds of individuals and I've asked the following question to put it in perspective. Here are a few examples of what financial success means to different people:

- Money isn't dictating any of your day-to-day actions.

- Not having to worry about if you'll have the money to cover a bill or buy a meal.

- Not having debts other than the usual costs of living (electric, phone, food, and so on).

- Doing something you want to do rather than you have to do.

- Supporting your family without depending on employment.

Achieving financial success means you are in control of your money, instead of it controlling you. You tell your dollars where to go, instead of them doing what they want to do. Your income doesn't necessarily determine how financially successful you are, your choices and priorities do. If you are struggling, financial success might seem like a distant dream.

The gist of the way John Maxwell used to put it was that success means knowing your purpose in life, and from that, growing to your maximum potential while sowing seeds that benefit others.

THOUGHT QUESTION

How do you define financial success?

MIND CHANGER

You can reverse poor thinking as well as the influence it has over your life by focusing on thoughts of freedom, determination, and pure will to position yourself for financial success!

9

The Wisdom to Know
Who You Are

Principle: You must know who you are to know what you are capable of achieving. You must know where you are to assess what's needed to proceed.

Muhammad Ali said, "I began calling myself the Greatest of All Time, hoping that eventually people would believe it." Now he'll go down in history as the greatest of all time, not because someone else called him that but because he said, "This is who I am"...so I ask you today...who are you?...who were you created to be?

I really don't like when the first question that someone asks is, "What do you do?" Why do you think that is the question most people ask? Is it just a habit? Are they programmed? Or maybe they don't have anything else to say. I truly believe the more appropriate question is, "What role do you play in this motion picture that we call life?" That's totally different than "What do you do?" The reality is, if you know *who* I am, you will find out not only what I do, but also why I do it. But many people want to hear and give the microwave quick answer, so it becomes, "I'm a doctor, I'm an attorney, I'm the vice president of a company, I'm a salesperson..." Sure, that is your title, but you are also so much more than a title. You are not what you do but who you were created to be. The problem is most people haven't thought about this question long enough to really have a definitive response. Think about it. The number-one question you've been asked since you were a kid is, "What do you want to be when you grow up?" This has been drilled into your subconscious, so it's only natural that you become what you do. You've never been asked, "Who are you?" But the reality is you must know who you are to know what you are capable of achieving.

I recently had an opportunity to attend The Steve and Marjorie Harvey Foundation Summer Camp in Texas. It is part of the Steve Harvey Mentoring Program for young men.

The goal of the program is to break the misguided habits of manhood and introduce young men to role models who provide positive examples of manhood. "The Steve Harvey Mentoring Weekend for Young Men" is a 4-day program designed to share and teach the principles of manhood to young men between the ages of 13 to 18, who live in a single, female-head-of-household home. This year I was one of those role models. I was excited about flying to Dallas to be a part of this weekend because I understood the challenges of being raised by a single female. What I didn't know is that I was in for an amazing growth opportunity that I didn't expect.

This program helps young men realize their potential and helps them to envision and prepare for a future in which they are strong, responsible, and productive men, so Mr. Harvey brings influential change makers from across the country to be a part of the 4-day, 3-night camp. This year, one of the influential figures was a man that I had been following for several years. His name is Michael V. Roberts, who in 1979, founded Roberts Properties, LLC, a multifaceted real estate and media enterprise he owns with his brother. The firm's portfolio consists of six properties located across St. Louis, including the Roberts Orpheum Theater, Roberts Lofts on the Plaza, Roberts Place Lofts, Roberts Place Homes, Roberts Tower, and Bahamas-based Roberts Isle. I had met Mr. Roberts about a year earlier at an awards ceremony but didn't have an opportunity to speak with him at length.

To my surprise, I'd get that opportunity in Texas. At the end of our first day of camp, which took place on Steve Harvey's ranch right outside of the Dallas–Fort Worth area, the guest speakers were being shuttled back to the hotel where we were staying. It was a long day and now the last shuttle was arriving to take four of us who were still hanging around camp back to the hotel.

The passengers that evening consisted of me; James Bailey, the CEO of Operation Hope, a National Economic Empowerment Organization; Nina Brown, a popular Atlanta radio producer; and Michael Roberts. The three of us piled in the back of the vehicle, while the elder statesman, Mr. Roberts, took the front passenger seat. We were all tired from a long day of activities, but I was also excited. I'd have a 30-minute ride back with a billionaire real estate developer and I had questions. I began asking Mr. Roberts about his upbringing in St. Louis and how he was able to build his wealth in the face of adversity that made poverty commonplace in the area he was raised.

As I prepared to engage him and ask his opinions, he turned around and asked the three of us in the back the same question one at a time. "Do you think outside of the box?" he asked. James quickly responded, "Yes, yes I do." Nina gave the same response, 'Yes, of course I think outside of the box." Next it was my turn, and almost before he could ask the question I said, "Yes, I do think outside of the box."

To our surprise, Mr. Roberts looked at us all and said, "I should come back there and spank you all!" Our faces dropped. We just knew we had the right answer. While we were eagerly awaiting an explanation, Mr. Roberts turned back around in his seat and said, "There is no box." He explained, "Society tells us there is a box to think outside of, so we create it."

This concept stuck with me. I realized that I and so many others I've encountered considered themselves forward thinkers, but we were all creating boxes. The reality is you create boxes and you allow others to put you in a box to make them feel better. They don't want you to try something that they haven't done before or known someone to do because it's the unknown. After all, if you could not rely on the baker to be a baker tomorrow, or the dentist to be a dentist, then the world would be in chaos, right? Well, that isn't your issue. You must realize that no one designs you; you design yourself. You determine how you will use what you've been given to make the "you" that you desire to be.

People will want to throw you back in the box because this is most convenient for them. Why? The bank wants you to keep your job to lend you money. Your family wants you to provide safety for them by being stable. Your friends don't want you to venture out because you might make a fool of yourself and bring ridicule on them as well. This problem plays out in a circle because our society places more weight on what someone does than who someone is.

When someone asks you, "Who are you?" you're inclined to give them your name. Your name is NOT who you are but is an easy label of identification. What I can tell you is "what" I do is not who I am...this is why so many lost themselves when the recent economic downturn left many without a job. You often associate your identity with your job and that can be dangerous. When the job is gone, you yourself become lost.

However, if you were to say, "I am going back to school to learn a new trade for the next 2 years, but I won't tell anyone what my new profession will be until I am finished," people would be confused and not know where to place you. If you don't believe me, try it. People and society need to put you into boxes to make themselves comfortable, and you allow them to do so. They don't want you to try something that amounts to the unknown. You then place restrictions on yourself by becoming only that by which others define you. Just think. If you could not rely on the postman to be a postman tomorrow, or the doctor to be a doctor, then do you think like them that the world would be in chaos?

For hundreds of years, people's identities have been tied to what they do. Many last names are derived from the profession of the person—Carpenter, Miller, Sawyer, Smith, and so on. You have become so accustomed to your professions being the source of your self-image and your names being the measure of who you are, you have lost your sense of something very important...yourself.

Are you independent, organized, light-hearted, creative, sensitive, analytical, a helper, a supporter, a problem-solver, a connector, a free spirit, or a lover of people? How would you describe yourself? What are the things that make you happy or provide joy to your life? I realize now that one question that I thought was so silly is a great way to begin to discover who you are when you identify what you would do for free. What do you love so much you would do it for free?

Time to Find You

Block out your career, your role as a mother, wife, husband, or father. Block out how much money you make or don't make; forget how successful or unsuccessful you are. If you're struggling with the question, you first need to know who you are beyond your name. When you know who are, a profession is only an extension of who you are. Make a list of things you love. What are the commonalities of those things? What are the common traits that surface in you while doing those things? Look at the list and attach some descriptive words. Use bold, expressive words that stir you like radical, extreme, encourager, influential, and fighter. These are closer to describing who you are than any profession could. Those traits in you have power, but the power is not in themselves, but in the proper combination with something that guides and activates them.

Your Purpose

Purpose pervades life, gives breath to life, like air.

Consciousness lets you aspire to loftier, meaning-based purposes. It lets you figure out what you were meant to do, and how to use your talents in service of that meaning. What makes a good meaningful purpose? It should be clear, concise, and specific, focused but flexible, energizing, and nourishing, rooted in love not fear, aligned with your fundamentals, especially your passions and desires, something you connect with emotionally, not just intellectually, grand and inspiring, and, most of all, worth building a life around.

To generate possible sources of meaningful purpose, answer these questions: What are your proudest accomplishments? What things in your life have made you feel complete, happy, or joy? What are your strengths? What are your passions? What do you want to change about you? Purpose is tied to passion. What do you believe your life's purpose is?

I spent many years letting those traits fly wildly or lay dormant in response to the environment around me. Regardless of the kind of people or situations, those traits could come out but were seldom guided. It is like going into a job just because you can meet the task requirements.

Being able to execute tasks is one thing, but having a framework that activates and guides who you are is another. In the wrong situation you feel stifled, frustrated, and disempowered because of the mismatch. Regardless of the tasks or title of a job, if it doesn't provide room for you, you'll never excel. The traits you carry around have enormous potential, or can cause huge amounts of damage if not guided and activated properly.

The key for me was understanding that the two most important days of my life were the day I was born and the day I discovered why I was born.

Your Journey

It's important to know yourself to reveal aspects of your character or psychological makeup to assist with planning and development. You must identify your strengths and the description of your personality type. You must discover the things that are most suitable for your personality type and the best businesses opportunities and direction to aid in implementing your plan. There are many aspects of the truth you hide from yourself because it would make you uncomfortable or remind you how you need to change now. Hidden truth actually cements negative situations in place. At the moment you finally own your truth, almost miraculously, positive change begins.

It's important to know yourself to reveal aspects of your character or psychological makeup to assist with planning and development. You must discover the things that are most suitable for your personality type and the best opportunities and direction to aid in implementing your plan.

Spoken truths always cause change that is positive in the long run, even if it's frightening at first.

THOUGHT QUESTION

What is that thing that is deep inside of you that has been suppressed because you've never explored it or given it a chance to develop outside of the confines of your current role?

MIND CHANGER

Your profession isn't the source of your self-image, nor is your name the measure of who you are. If this is the case, you have lost your sense of something very important: yourself.

10

Where Would You Like to Go?

Principle: When you can see your destination, it's a lot easier to get there.

One day I was outside with my 7-year-old daughter. I turned to her with a challenge. "Let's race," I said in my competitive daddy voice. She then looked back at me and asked the most important question that you forget to ask when it comes to your finances. "Where are we racing to?"

Do you start things without knowing what the end looks like or where it is? How can you know if you've arrived at your destination if you haven't designated one? Do you believe that whatever sense of fulfillment you are missing will be achieved by arriving at some place in the future? Or that the power to create it exists outside of what's already available to you? You go on missing life in the present, so the future becomes your hope for a better life. Tomorrow never comes because all you have is the present moment. You are always in the present moment. You just go on missing out because your attention is always focused on a future destination.

Set Your Goals

I believe the essence of life is to have a dream or a goal. Actively pursuing something of importance is the very thing that will make you feel alive, young, stimulated, and happy.

Creating a plan of action with clear, specific goals is the key to achieve what you want. You must know exactly what you desire to achieve. Write down every detail with as much description as you can. The process of writing the goals down and putting everything into words gives you clarity to keep a vivid image of it in your mind. Then when you read through that description later, you'll remember exactly where you were headed and remain motivated.

The key to not get overwhelmed is to break down huge goals into smaller steps. You might have heard the saying that you can't eat the whole elephant in one bite, but if you take smaller portions over time, you will eventually devour it. This applies to your goals as well. Maybe you've set up a major goal you're working toward, but now it's time to break it down a bit. First start by creating a few big milestones along the way, and then break those down even further until you have a bunch of little steps to walk along.

Ask yourself the following:

- What are the steps you could take to help you move toward your goals?

- In what sequence do those steps need to be? What are the actions that need to be done every day to keep you on the right track toward the goal?

When you figure out the answers to these questions, it will be easier to create an action plan. For example, if you want to pay off your credit card debt, you need to first figure out how much you owe and then create a solid set of actions that can help you gather the money to pay off that debt.

You must also make a list of your personal strengths in relation to your goal. For instance, if you have an earning goal, you might want to consider strengths like your level of commitment to working your plan and doing the tasks to make that a reality. It might be that you enjoy cooking and you are an excellent cook. The list of personal strengths you can draw up is endless.

You must define and describe your goal. Write down when you want to achieve it. Write down the reasons why you want it. Write down what it would feel like after you have achieved it and write down your accomplished goals. Figure out exactly what it will take to get it. Be realistic about the time things will take. Many people don't allow themselves enough time and give up too soon.

Here's a goal-setting method to help you set the goals that can help you reach the level of success you envision:

> **Workable:** Can you realistically handle your plan? Can it produce the desired effect or result? Don't create a plan that can easily be broken. If you have been experiencing a shortage in what you need to cover your survival for some time, don't expect changes to happen overnight. Take your time and understand this will be a lifestyle change for you. Remember your mind is a powerful tool. If you set standards too high at first and you stumble, it will

be harder for you to get back up and start again. A goal that can actually be accomplished is realistic.

Empowering: Can you remain strong to accomplish your plan to prioritize your spending? Will your plan improve your current situation and help you take control of your life? Things happen, but this is why willpower and discipline are crucial for a successful execution of your plan. Having words of affirmation and declaration posted on your bathroom mirror or on your desk while you work can help remind you of your plan to overcome your desire to overspend and succeed. A goal that gives you strength can enable you to move closer to achieving desired results.

Asset-producing: Does your plan allow you to do other things with your money? How will it increase your current asset position? If you curb your spending and prioritize your spending to take care of survival needs first, you might have enough left over to save for investments or other financial growth opportunities. Let your money finally work for you, instead of the opposite. A goal that provides an advantage or benefit to your life can be leveraged.

Leverage-able: Can you measure the success of your plan? Will your plan take you from where you are to where you want to be? Stay on track and see if your plan is making a difference in your spending and personal bottom line. If you find that you have been curbing unnecessary spending and you still remain short to cover survival needs, it might be time to evaluate your plan to see what needs to be tweaked. Maybe some of your survival needs can be downsized with better rates from other companies that offer services you need with a lower price point. A goal that can be measured will determine if it yields the appropriate results you desire based on the output of your efforts.

Time-sensitive: Are you giving yourself proper time to achieve success? How long will it take you to have the results you desire? Don't stress yourself out if things don't work out for you like you planned in the beginning. Don't allow yourself to get lazy in your execution either. You know yourself better than anyone, and you know how you are wired financially. With this in mind, allocate enough time to achieve your desired results and watch your progression. Time is a valuable commodity. Don't abuse it. Use it. If you can, push yourself as far as you can go and do what it takes to get your personal financial life zone in order. A goal that allocates enough time to be achieved will determine the value of success.

Harvestable: Can you change the trajectory of your current financial situation? Will your plan take you from where you are to where you desire to be?

Now visualize. Close your eyes and imagine yourself accomplishing your goals. Where are you? How did you get there? How do you feel? Do this often. Don't get swayed by the noise and happenings going on outside. Put your attention on what you are working to achieve. Remember your goal, and you will have control over the discomforts and difficulties.

- Brainstorm ideas. Are there different ways to reach your goal? Write everything down that you can think of in 3 minutes, no matter how silly or impossible it might seem.

- Revisit, evaluate, and if necessary, adjust your goals. Keep a written record of your goals in a place where you'll remember to read them every day.

Vision

A vision statement is a compass that guides you to a destination you have set for yourself in life. It ensures that you stay focused on your plan to achieve your goals and keeps you on track so that you do not deviate from the course you have set. It is a guiding light and a beacon to lead you through storms and rocky terrain toward your destination.

Without a personal vision statement, most people tend to become aimless drifters in life. They have no definite goals for the future and no long-term direction.

Without direction, you will be caught up with short-term outcomes like paying the bills, watching your favorite TV shows, going shopping, going through the daily motions, and generally just trying to survive the rat race. You will be caught up in a stressed and monotonous existence instead of designing your destiny and truly living.

What does a vision do for you?

Your personal vision statement will usually be derived from your personal value system and beliefs. Values are traits or qualities that are considered worthwhile; they represent your highest priorities and deeply held driving forces. You usually stay true to your values and, therefore, it is important to develop your personal vision statement from the perspective of your values:

- A personal vision statement makes it easier to develop the objectives, milestones, and strategies that will help you achieve your vision.

- A personal vision statement acts as a yardstick against which you can measure your current situation and your progress.

- A personal vision statement also allows you to evaluate your values. If, for example, one of your values is integrity, you will know when you are compromising the fulfillment of your vision if you are acting without integrity.

A few examples of values are honesty, ambition, competency, individuality, integrity, responsibility, respect, dedication, loyalty, credibility, efficiency, dignity, empathy, accomplishment, courage, wisdom, independence, influence, friendliness, order, generosity, optimism, dependability, and flexibility.

Keep in mind that your personal vision statement is a look into the future. It defines what and who you want to become at a set time in the future. It should not be vague, or else you cannot develop a strategy to achieve it.

Now write your personal vision statement. Use the preceding information to craft your personal vision statement.

Write in the first person and make statements about the future you want to achieve. Be specific, set goals you want to achieve, set a time frame, and articulate the statements in such a way that they can be evaluated and measured.

Your Vision Statement:

_____

_____

_____

_____

_____

_____

THOUGHT QUESTION

What helps you see your vision so clearly that it appears to be right before you?

MIND CHANGER

Remember, you are in control of your own life and have the power to make changes. It doesn't matter where you are as long as you are willing to make a change and ready to do something about it.

11

Why Do You Want It?

hat is that thing that you want so bad you can taste it? What is the driving force behind you getting up every morning to pound the pavement, answer those phones, work long hours, take those orders, or do the presentation? You must have a strong desire to win! If you choose to just be, and operate on autopilot, you are setting yourself up for failure. Do you realize that all thought first begins with desire? Desires are basically the intangible feeling you get when you have an unfulfilled want or need. What you desire the most is usually what you will think about the most and therefore draw into your life. Many of the thoughts you have on a daily basis are random thoughts that serve as triggers that prompt negative and anxious emotions, usually causing stress. These thoughts are stored in your mind waiting for an opportunity to rear their ugly heads often.

Why do you want to get your financial life in order? Is it to achieve financial security and freedom that can change lives? Why do you want to be able to save? So you can eventually spend more, or to be prepared for the things you must purchase in life? Why do you want better credit? Is it to to buy more things, or move your family into a better school district and purchase a home with the best interest rate? Why do you want to start a business? Is it to just say that you have a business, or is it to make your mark on the world and improve lives or fill a void in the marketplace? Why do you want to be wealthy for that matter? Until you discover your "why," you might be doing things for the wrong reason. In essence, you have no purpose outside of having more. In an age in which more is better as you look to be super-sized and have instant gratification, that should be enough, right? Wrong!

Until you explore your "why," you're stuck in a perpetual state of going through the motions usually for the wrong reasons. Is your family the reason you wake up every morning to get to work early to earn the paycheck? Is it to purchase that thing you've been wanting all your life? Is it to show others that you can accomplish a goal? Is it to prove to yourself that you can do what you set your mind to? Is it to provide for your parents in their old age? Is it to live by example and show others what is truly possible? Whatever your reason might be, the key is to have a reason. Know what your "why" is to give your quest purpose and eliminate the thoughts that don't contribute to your progression.

When posed with this question, I realized that it wasn't just enough to say I needed to earn money or to provide for my family. Why did I want to provide for my family? Is it because society tells me that's what I'm supposed to do as a man? Or is it that I want them to see the values of a good work ethic, to be cared for financially to have a better life, and possibly to begin to build generational wealth that will allow them to enjoy life and broaden their horizons. That's my "why" that I keep before me and renew daily. So what's your "why?"

If you could get clear enough to find your "why" before you take your next step, I wonder how much abundance would flow into your life. When you don't know why you are acting, choosing, or moving in one direction or another, there's no passion, reason, or purpose in your life!

If you don't know your "why,"

- You can't be clear and centered and make the best decisions for your own life.

- You often feel stuck. You procrastinate. You get cluttered in your mind.

- You aren't being pulled toward your goals by your inspiration. Instead, you are simply going through the motions.

When I decided to venture out and start my own business, I had many people who were close to me try to talk me out if it. The main ones talking me out of it were individuals who had never taken a risk in their lives. I understood they weren't talking me out of it because they didn't want to see me succeed, but rather they felt they had my best interest at heart. Many refer to this group of persuaders as dream-stealers because you often become discouraged and apprehensive about living your dreams after being told that you shouldn't. During the startup years it was rough, to say the least, but in essence it was one of the most rewarding, character-building experiences in my life.

In the midst of the process, the bills were mounting and my savings had been exhausted. The thing that kept me going was the DESIRE to succeed. It was sheer willpower that pushed me and told me to keep going. I felt that this had become my calling. I realized that challenges were inevitable, but if I had a strong will to make it work, I would be able to make it through. I had made a decision to push through no matter what it looked like. I was embracing the attitude that whatever didn't kill me would ultimately make me stronger.

Do you desire positive thoughts or do you desire to fill your mind with negative thoughts? You might be saying you can't help but think about the things that are wrong because you're working to fix them. I've created a process to refocus, reshape, and renew your mind to reverse those negative thoughts to meet the demands of life and avoid the negative items that spread and keep you frozen.

You must realize that your mind and your finances must be connected; this link begins with your thoughts. You don't have to allow the negative thoughts to invade your brain and body and affect your financial life. You have the power to control these thoughts, but without the proper planning, self-control, and discipline, you leave yourself exposed and susceptible to a negative thought process.

Imagine that you are self-employed and need additional customers to earn the funds needed to keep the lights on. If you focus on the fact that you don't have the money now to get the lights turned on, rather the actions needed to acquire the money, you won't be able to carry out the plan to meet the need. You are using valuable brain power and energy thinking about the issue rather than thinking about the solution.

Your desires lead to thoughts that lead to decisions and ultimately actions, but the desire is the trigger that starts the chain reaction. You must realize that you're always making a decision. Whether it's deciding to move or stand still, a decision was made because deciding to do nothing is still a decision.

Too often we skip our thoughts, feelings, and the psychology of our personal financial success and go right to implementing theories, practices, and concepts that we don't even know are right for our situations, personality, or thought processes. We begin ventures that sound good or invest in things that we don't love nor have the capacity to build. Therefore, we find that budgeting, saving, and investing methods fail. Not because they are faulty, but because we haven't taken the time to prepare mentally and explore our "whys." We haven't explored why we really want to achieve our goals, or overcome our obstacles, and accumulate wealth, and achieve success. What's our reason for wanting success anyway? Why do we get up and go to work every day?

For this connection to be made, it has to be for more than a paycheck. You have to internalize your thoughts and know what works best for your situation. Similar to a diet, just because it works for one person doesn't mean the same diet will work for you as well.

You are not alone. All over the world people deal with uncontrolled desires that lead to brokenness, lack of funds, and bad credit, all to realize unfulfilled dreams or wants that they tell themselves are needs. The reality is that some deal with it better than others and thrive. Many people experience success because they have created a system in their minds to overcome these obstacles to focus on what's important. In other words, they know how to focus on the main thing and develop a plan that allows them to realize the dream.

Negative desires or unrealistic desires give birth to foul or unrealistic thoughts, which translate into stress. You can't be double-minded and focus on what's wrong and work to improve the situation at the same time. This doesn't mean you shouldn't acknowledge what is wrong in your life, but you shouldn't focus just on the problem. Instead, you must be solution-centered and develop a methodology that propels you to where you want to go in life.

Your "why" is your inspired reason.

People who find their "why" improve their focus, and then they attract more success and abundance! When you come from a place of inspiration, then you know you have found your "why." If you are taking action because it feels good, you have found your "why." When you are crystal clear that the step you are about to take is right for you, you have found your "why." Remember, the Law of Attraction sends you situations that have the same energy and vibration you are putting out. So, when you are feeling inspired and confident because you know how to find your "why," the universe will bring you more opportunities that match this energetic feeling.

THOUGHT QUESTION

What is your "why?"

MIND CHANGER

Your "why" must be bigger than a paycheck

12

Your Assets

Principle: You must identify and use your nonmonetary assets to achieve your goals.

I often begin my seminars by asking people if they believe they are wealthy. The majority of people don't raise their hands because they don't believe they possess enough money to be considered wealthy. You might not have much money, but did you know that you have assets that you can exchange for money? The truth is money isn't the only asset that has value. You are likely sitting on assets that are more valuable than money because of the potential to convert them to cash is unlimited. Anything tangible or intangible that can be owned or controlled to produce value, and that is held to have positive economic value, is considered an asset. Think for a few moments about what things you might possess that fit that description. The truth is you usually take better care of items that you paid for rather than things you got for free, such as the assets we'll discuss.

In this chapter, you consider a few nonmonetary assets, such as Time, Relationships, Gifts/Talents, Ambition, Applied Knowledge, and Dreams/Ideas, and how they can be applied to your life to help you reach your financial goals.

Time

Principle: Time is more valuable than money; invest it wisely.

Time is a curious asset, good economically, yet fragile in other ways, too. It is highly perishable. Were it a bank account, time would pay no interest, close itself out each night, carry over no balances, and allow no overdrafts. What does that mean for the value of time? It is also tradable in many ways. We can reallocate time, but we can't increase our supply. I can shop for food rather than grow food myself (or order in dinner rather than cook), using the time I save to undertake higher value activities that will let me pay for my outsourcing.

86,400

As you measure the durations of events and the intervals between them, you must realize you have 86,400 seconds in each day. You need to learn to manage them to achieve your goals. To be a good steward over your time you must explore time management techniques that help you maximize your time and get the results you desire. You must identify how much time it takes you to complete your daily commitments, how much time you have available after commitments to fill in other activities, how much time you waste daily, weekly, and monthly, identify non-income-producing activities, and identify income-producing activities and potential income-producing activities.

If each one of those 86,400 seconds in each day were a dollar, you would invest wisely and look for some sort of return on each of those seconds. You should be looking for a ROTI (return on time invested). Just like money, it's okay to give some away to those in need, but you have to decide how much you can give.

The Price of Time

The U.S. Mint prints about $600 million dollars daily. In all my years, I have yet to find a time factory that makes more time. Have you found that? If you have, please tell me where it is. Time is the most valuable commodity. We never seem to have enough of it. Everyone is time-strapped, time-poor, or time-starved. Choose your cliché. Why don't we value time as we do any other good or service? Many of us think we have an abundance of time, especially when we are young, but the older we get, we begin, or should begin, to see that the clock moves rapidly.

You must price your time.

You don't earn as much as you think you do. You might be paid $15 an hour, but your real hourly wage is less than that. Possibly much less. Say you have a friend named Mike and that he's an electrician making approximately $48,000 a year for a 40-hour work week. His nominal wage is approximately $24 per hour. Ah, but it's not that simple. Mike's real hourly wage isn't $24. It's something lower when you account for his hidden expenses associated with the job.

Not only is knowing your real hourly wage useful in terms of budgeting both your time and money, but it's also a great tool for comparing opportunities. Even two jobs that offer the same salary in different neighborhoods and cities can have big differences in terms of real hourly wage. I stopped doing certain things when I determined what my hourly rate was. For example, I don't cut my lawn anymore because I can pay someone $25 dollars to do that and my hourly rate is significantly higher. Now if I truly enjoyed the outdoors and the act of cutting and smelling fresh cut grass, I would do it. I rarely watch TV because I'm not being compensated for that. I pick and choose how I will use my time and always ask myself the question: How will spending this time bring value to my life?

I make how much?

I have a friend who has a job she loves and makes about $50,000 a year, but her job causes her to do a lot of extra things and be at events that are after regular work hours. So she began to calculate her hourly rate and realized it was about $7/hour. This was an eye-opening experience for her.

Quantify all the expenses and time associated with your job. Think of all the things you do and the money you spend that you wouldn't if you did not work.

Managing Your Time Well

There are many things that I no longer do because I have determined what my hourly rate is. For example, if my hourly rate is $100 and I watch 3 hours of TV a day, I'm losing $300 a day. The people on TV are getting paid to be there and I'm losing money, so I rarely watch TV. I love clothes, but hate shopping—the going to multiple stores and looking all over to buy something. I just want to go in, get what I need, and come out. Now, if it takes me 3 hours to find what I'm looking for, and then I have to pay $200 to purchase it, what has that item truly cost me? If you said $500, you are correct.

Quantify all the expenses and time associated with your job. Think of all the things you do and the money you spend that you wouldn't if you did not work. Subtract your work-related expenses from your annual salary to find your actual earnings.

Work Related Expense – Annual Salary = Actual Earnings

Divide your actual earnings by the total number of hours you spend each year on work-related tasks (including business trips, office social events, commuting, and so on).

How many hours you truly work: _____

Think about how much time your expenditures are actually costing you. Remember that time is money.

Time management is a key element of a calm mindset. When you know what's expected of you and when, you can better plan for and address every need.

Time Blocking

Time blocking is an effective strategy for using time wisely and being more productive. This is a useful skill for you if you feel like you juggle multiple tasks and either don't manage your tasks or your time well. Therefore, you need structure to make the most of each day. Blocking out time for specific activities allows you to focus on one task at a time, limiting distractions, procrastination, and stress. Here are some strategies for effective time blocking.

Time Blocking Tips

- Identify your high-priority tasks and projects. Time blocking is especially effective for tasks requiring greater concentration.

- Block out time for specific tasks. Break tasks down into chunks that can be completed in smaller time increments.

- Set a goal to finish the task within the time allotted. Decide on start and finish times for the particular task and adhere to the schedule.

- Limit activities that interfere with your time-blocking goals.

- Eliminate unproductive, time-consuming activities.

- Find quiet work spots. A coffee shop, a library. or a quiet corner of your office building are possible places to spend uninterrupted blocks of time focused on specific tasks.

- Block time by yourself to complete tasks that require greater thought and concentration. Scheduling time alone can help you focus on challenging tasks.

- Use a visual tool to block time. Your visual aide might be a calendar, a piece of paper, or an Excel spreadsheet. Mark the blocks of time to show clear start and stop times.

- Draw blocks of time on a piece of paper. Write a short description of each task in each time block. Draw a line through the task when completed.

- Schedule breaks. Regular breaks are conducive to greater productivity and concentration.

Relationships

Principle: Who you know can help leverage what you know to identify opportunities.

Did you realize having a lot of relationships and not knowing how to manage them are like having a lot of money and not knowing how to manage it?

I have two friends who call me often. One friend calls and always ask for something. "Can I have...? Will you help me...? Will you send me...?" I also have a friend who calls to check on me. He always asks questions like, "Are you okay? Do you need any help?" Because he knows I travel often, he also asks if I'm eating right. Which call do you think I'll pick up first? If you guessed the second friend who's always looking to add value, you're right. It's human nature. If you are always taking from someone, eventually they will become empty and have nothing left to give. My friend who desires to add value asks these questions because he understands the principle. To withdraw, you must first deposit.

You must realize that building valuable relationships is not just passing out business cards. Whether you realize or not, relationships are the fuel that feeds the success of your life/business. Here's how to make ones that last. Successful long-term relationships involve ongoing effort and compromise by two or more individuals. Building healthy patterns early in your relationship can establish a solid foundation. I am going to suggest to you the management of something which I think is very important and very much ignored: your circle of friends, or better yet, the design of the circle of your friends.

You Must Deposit Before You Can Withdraw

I think many people are unclear on the concept of how true relationships are created. I recently had a young lady express her frustration with the notion of mentors. She stated that she had reached out to several people to ask them to mentor her, but they were all either too busy or many just never responded to her request.

By the time she reached me, she was disillusioned with the whole concept and asked, "How am I supposed to find a mentor if no one will help me?" After hearing this I asked, "What have you been asking the people you contacted?"

She explained that she was sending them a message, explaining who she was, what she was studying, and why she thought the person would be a great mentor for her. I listened as she continued to express that she believed they should respond to her because they have a duty to give back and help others. "How will I ever learn if no one helps me!?" she bellowed in frustration.

I explained that it sounded like she had been reaching out to the right people. "You want them to mentor you because they are busy," I said, "which is an indication that they are in demand in their specific field of expertise." She agreed, so I continued, "But you are going about it all wrong. Have you ever gone into a bank and were able to withdraw money before you've ever made one deposit?"

"No," she replied.

"Well, think about the individuals who you are contacting as if they were banks. How can you truly expect someone to give up their time, which is one of their most valuable assets, to help you, when you haven't made any deposits into their life?"

She continued to look at me like I wasn't making sense. So I explained to her that even though I was on CNN, I would still contact people I knew who were authors and on the speaking circuit to travel with them to help them however I could. I would help them sell books after they spoke, make sure their area was prepared to receive customers and answer questions, but before I even did this I always did my homework to know exactly what their needs were so I could deliver value. If I didn't know what their needs were, there was no way I could make a deposit.

I would always receive invaluable information, lessons, stories, and tips from providing my services because we would usually debrief over a great meal because we both felt like we had received value. This lesson has proved to help me on many levels. I always make sure I'm making a deposit and offering something valuable in exchange for anyone's time, knowledge, or resources. The reality is that no one owes you anything. You must deliver value to get it in exchange.

Creating a Circle of W.E.A.L.T.H.

This is why I suggest to you the management of your circle of friends, or the design of your circle of friends. Think about it: Every week you spend quite a few hours with your friends. The proper circle of friends for you can be a lot more than a bunch of people you hang out with or tweet to. Having the right friends can mean

- Fun experiences together; you look forward to every time.

- A powerful connection, based on your core common points.

- A deep sense of respect and appreciation for each other.

- The ability to be comfortable, authentic, and open with them.

- Knowing you have your back covered by great people.

In practice, few people experience these kinds of things with their friends. I believe this happens a lot because most people build their circle of friends in a reactive way. They happen to meet some people in school, at work, at different activities; they interact because of the context and eventually, they get used to each other and become friends.

Here are a few tips to help you build your relationships and create your Circle of Influence:

- Listen more than you speak.

- Encourage honest feedback.

- It's not always about what you can get but also what you can give. Offer help.

- Keep notes on everyone you meet, use key words to describe them or things they like, and search your database for key words to find all the people that have the same words.

- Remember birthdays, anniversaries, and special moments.

- A friend that always calls to ask for something...and a friend that always calls to offer something.

- Be sure to contact people when you are NOT in need of something.

- Take time to learn about their likes/dislikes because they are as important to them as yours are to you.

- Understand the dreams of others and provide opportunities for them to fulfill this whenever possible.

Living Database

Because your network/database is alive, you have to do something every day, and the care and feeding of your network will be alive and well. Here are a few options that might help you stay organized:

- Outlook

- Mac Mail

- Constant Contact

- Mail Chimps

- Excel

People appreciate that you are looking out for them:

- Connect often.

- Send thank-you notes as soon as you meet someone...stand out (personalized note cards...include a business card).

- Be a connector...find opportunities for others...it's not always about you.

- Go deeper...not just on the surface.

- Be proactive.

Use your journal and knowledge of your relationships, and forward articles, links, and other information that might be of interest to your contacts.

Devise a system to ensure that not too much time passes before you connect with your contacts. With the proliferation of social media tools these days such as Facebook, LinkedIn, and Twitter, it's never been easier to keep in touch.

Tips

- Keep it real! Be yourself...don't put on airs.
- Be an effective communicator.
- Meet face to face when you can...nothing like it.
- Promote honest exchanges.

List current relationships or have them in a database; classify your relationships.

What you need to do is proactively build your circle of friends, by following a couple steps.

Decide What You Want

This is the crucial starting point: deciding the key traits you want your friends to have. This step allows you to filter the people you interact with and the time you dedicate to each one, to maximize the positive outcomes.

Pick up a pen and paper, and actually write down these traits, after you think about them really well. But make sure you don't write too many traits; otherwise, you'll create such a strong filter you'll end up with no friends.

Get Out There

After you decide what kind of people you want to befriend, it's time to go out and meet them. Start thinking about the kind of places and activities where you have the best chances of meeting people fitting your desired profile, and get involved.

Trim the Fat

It's also important to cut down on the interactions with people who are already in your social circle and you realize they do not really fit the friend profile you're looking for. Otherwise, especially if you also need a decent amount of alone time like me, you will have little time for finding and interacting with people you enjoy more.

As you work through this process, some of the people you start seeing less of might judge you or blame you for being distant. Don't feel bad about doing this. Just move on and keep doing what you're doing. With time, as you build a truly awesome circle of friends for yourself, all these little things will no longer matter.

Following are fundamental techniques in making valuable connections with people:

- Don't criticize, condemn, or complain.

- Give honest and sincere appreciation.

- Arouse in the other person an eager want.

Six ways to make people like you follow:

- Become genuinely interested in other people.

- Smile.

- Remember that a person's name is to that person the sweetest and most important sound in any language.

- Be a good listener. Encourage others to talk about themselves.

- Talk in terms of the other person's interests.

- Make the other person feel important—and do it sincerely.

Relationships can help take you closer to your goal if managed correctly. You must remember that this is a form of currency, so protect and value your relationships and they will pay off.

Natural Abilities

Principle: You must identify your gifts and talents and discipline yourself to continually grow and use them to achieve the success you desire.

Is talent born or made? The dictionary says talent is a "natural endowment" of a person, so you're born with your talents. Imagine if you had someone to help you focus on those talents from the time you were born, discovered them, and then helped you know how to apply them? Because that is probably not the case, it's up to you to grow and develop them.

Talent is an ability or natural capacity or potential that we have, which might range from our creativity or intellect or social skills to our athletic abilities. We all have talents, but we're not always so good at identifying what they are. In fact, our best talents can be right in front of us, and we miss them. We're so busy searching for a talent we think is hot or lucrative, or sexy or fun, or more like how we imagine our life being, that we overlook the actual tremendous potential we have sitting there waiting to be discovered.

Identify Your Talents

If you can determine what your talents are, you can tap into an amazing resource that can help you in every aspect of your life, including your business. Whether you are searching for the perfect type of business to open or you want to find ways to grow the one you have, you might find the answer in your personal talents.

Talents are different from skills, in that they tend to be innate rather than learned. When found, they can be nurtured and developed, but finding them can be tricky. It's partly a process of self-observation and honesty. The rest is learning and practice. Talents can come in many varieties. They might be artistic or technical, mental or physical, or inwardly or outwardly directed. They need not be profitable, useful, or conventional, but they will always be your own, part of what makes you, you.

You must be open-minded and patient. Remember that you don't need to practice forever. At some point, develop something worth showing the world, and show it. When you maximize the gifts and talents that you have been given, you will begin fulfilling your purpose and become great in your chosen field of expertise.

Go Deeper

With pad and pen, take inventory of your skills and abilities.

What activities are you currently doing that can be eliminated to maximize your Time Asset?

I asked a thousand people this question: If you received a call from Caller (A) who always calls to ask for something and another call simultaneously from Caller (B) who always calls to give you something, which call would you answer? No one chose A.

13

Leverage

Principle: You must use your assets wisely to achieve your goal.

The Seesaw

Imagine a seesaw; you know, the wooden kind that they used to have at the park. On one side you see boxes with all your assets inside and each box is labeled. You see your Time, Relationships, Gifts and Talents, and so on. On the other side you see a stack of money that appears to be the heaviest of the two because it is weighted down to the ground while your box of assets sits on the other side elevated. Although the money keeps your assets elevated, there appears to be a force field surrounding the money that makes it impossible to touch. You quickly learn that boxes are sitting there empty and to add weight to that side of the seesaw, you must input your assets. The more assets you put in, the higher the money side increases, and the cage begins to lift and make the funds accessible. This is exactly how this seesaw concept works on the playground. The plank that the money and assets sit on is the leverage used to find balance or tilt the weight to the appropriate or desired side. In this case, the weight needs to shift to the asset side to increase the cash.

Establish Clearly Defined Direction and Priorities

A good plan outlines a clearly defined direction that includes supporting objectives, goals, and measures and details your desired results. A good plan also identifies a few set of strategic priorities. This level of focus helps make executing your plan much easier.

Unfortunately, most plans are written at a high level, making it difficult to know how to put it into action effectively. To deal with this, you must take the time to personalize your strategy. This means communicating your plan into clearly defined, actionable terms so you can actually see yourself completing the task in the strategic plan. You must create a map to serve as a visual communication tool that you use to draw a picture of your financial success creation plan, which includes your values, goals, vision, and strategy in the form of steps to be accomplished to get you closer to achieving your goals. You, as well as those that must help you follow the plan, must see the plan in action.

This map enables you to communicate the priority of the various objectives in the plan. When done right, this plan can guide the financial decisions of all those in your family or home who must follow this strategy on a daily basis. It helps them determine where to best focus the resources or assets available to them.

Why Leverage?

The purpose of leverage is to use what you have to get you where you desire to go. You must create a comprehensive evaluation negotiating the financial barriers that inevitably arise in every stage of life.

So now examine a series of steps for an individual or business with which you can organize your finances, and design a blueprint using your assets to ensure you accomplish your financial goals for earning, spending, and saving current and future income.

Often it's too difficult to see through your mess to see what's right in front of you. This usually occurs because you are tripped up by your past mistakes or stuck at the pit stop in the town of "reality." One of the biggest mistakes you can make is spending or investing without a plan. Without a plan, you're prone to make mistakes and experience setbacks. Because of these setbacks, you might not think winning is possible, mainly because you can't see past what's before you now. Your situation seems so big it blocks your view of the future. Because of this block, you might be short on vision, and without vision, you're blind. If successful people listened to the negative press, comments, and all the naysayers that said they were sure to lose, it would affect their psyche and decrease the probability of reaching their goal. The key is to block the negativity, choose your direction, and choose it wisely. Have a definite desire of what you actually want life to pay because it's willing to give you what you ask of it.

Thinking of a Master Plan

Financial planning is the long-term process of wisely managing your finances so that you can achieve your goals and dreams, while at the same time negotiating the financial barriers that inevitably arise in every stage of life. The method for planning that I have found to be most effective is to create a schedule and stick to it. During any period of time on the schedule, you may think only about the subject in question. For example, if you have scheduled reading a financial book for a period in your schedule, then you must stick to reading the book. You may not eat, pee, sleep, accept phone calls, or anything else. This sounds extreme, but it builds your feelings so that ignoring distractions becomes second nature to you.

Creating the master plan is a crucial step in reaching your desired results. Following are five key steps to formulating your plan. Regardless of the purpose for the plan, it must cover five key areas:

1. What is the goal or the end result?

2. What do you need to do to get there (steps/objectives)?

3. How do you plan to accomplish it (action plan)?

4. How long will it take you to accomplish these steps or how much time have you allowed to accomplish the steps (measurement/time)?

5. What resources and tools do you have to help get you there?

Imagine that you're preparing to build a new home. You've had many experiences through the years that have taught you lessons, and also you've had ideas of what the perfect home would look like. Before construction begins, you sit down with your builder to review your design goals. You ask when you can see the blueprints, but he tells you he doesn't use blueprints, but rather likes to design as he goes. He feels that blueprints are restricting, so he doesn't use them.

The odds are you probably wouldn't hire a builder that did that. It's a proven fact that when building a house, it's good to have a blueprint or plan of action that outlines what's needed, the steps, the materials, and the time to complete before beginning the task. The bigger the goals, the more planning is needed. Unfortunately, you might be operating without a plan; even though you think you have it in your head, you actually don't have a plan and have chosen to operate by default rather than on purpose or intentionally.

Why would you take something as important as building a solid financial future for granted or leave it to chance? Where you are financially currently is by design or lack of design. Many people don't stop to think about this until it's too late and their financial lives are in ruin, which is where most realize a plan is needed. You cannot nor should you make any financial decisions independent of a master plan.

Now is the time to allocate some time to create a personalized Financial Success Plan that's designed to build the kind of financial future you envision.

This chapter is designed to help you create a plan that works for you. There is no cookie cutter answer, but this blueprint can help you by providing the key components and customizing a solution for yourself. For this plan to work, you have to revisit the chapter on goals to make sure you have identified clearly defined goals to establish your financial priorities.

List your goals. Create a spending plan, or what some people call a budget, which is an essential tool for everyone, no matter how much money they have. Without a spending plan, you can't intelligently implement saving and investing strategies because you don't know if you have any gaps or a surplus in your plan. Therefore, you can't make informed financial decisions.

Your personal financial goals and budget reflect how you view and use your assets. Married couples should make these planning decisions together because it establishes you as a team rather than opponents. One-half of marriages end in divorce, and 80 percent of those are due, in part, to money problems. Jointly establishing a financial plan helps create a foundation for a solid financial future and can potentially help save your marriage.

The following are key components that you should include in your plan, but you can make adjustments where needed to customize it for your financial life:

1. Make a Financial Success Plan, relying on your current spending to establish realistic initial estimates in each category. You must track your expenses carefully to ensure your spending plan uses realistic figures.

2. Establish your short- and medium-term financial goals. Then look at your budget to determine if your available surplus puts you in a position to

realize your goals. Or if you have a gap that needs to be filled either by changing positions for one with a larger salary or looking at ways to create additional streams of income.

3. Get realistic estimates of how much money you'll need to retire. Sound Mind Investing (SMI)'s Retirement Planning Worksheet Calculator (www. soundmindinvesting.com/tools/) can help you with this task, as can many of the other good calculators available at other financial websites. Having specific figures in mind can help motivate you if you need to start saving more, or potentially keep you off the austerity budget if you're doing better than you thought. Attack your debt, while avoiding further debt. This might not be easy, but it's worth it. It doesn't make much sense to be paying high interest rates while you attempt to save because the high interest rates cancel out your savings.

4. List all your debts, including balances and interest rates. You have a choice: You can begin with the debt with the highest interest rate first, so you aren't throwing your money out of the window, or you can begin with the lowest balance. Paying the lowest debt gives you a sense of accomplishment and helps you become motivated to keep going. If seeing your debts disappear keeps you motivated, it's worth paying a little extra interest.

5. Start building your W.E.A.L.T.H. fund by opening a high-yielding interest account and having money automatically deposited into it each month.

6. Take advantage of your retirement plan up to the amount your company matches. If you're deep in debt, skip this step for now. But if your debt is manageable, meaning you have a clear plan to pay it off reasonably soon, take advantage of employer matching in your 401(k) or other retirement plan if it's available.

7. Fund a Roth Individual Retirement Account (IRA). This is an incredible tool. You'll get at least 20+ years of compound growth and then get to take that money out tax-free!

After you get your strategy set up and going, continue to follow it no matter what. Don't let current events (and the emotions surrounding them) interrupt your plan.

Following are a few other key things to consider:

- Start a college savings account. If you already have a child, the clock is ticking on their education savings. Consider using a life insurance policy for your child, Section 529 plan, Coverdell Education Account, or even Roth IRA.

- Create an investment strategy to determine how much money you'd like to invest for the future. Remember that you never invest with money you need to live or meet obligations.

- Explore where you can cut expenses. Look at services you don't use often, call creditors to ask them to reduce interest rates, and shop for the best insurance rates annually.

- Pull a copy of your credit report at **www.annual-creditreport.com** at least one time a year to include this in the plan.

- Negotiate the best rate to eliminate old debt.

- Keep your affirmations as a part of your plan.

- Review relationships often to determine if you have individuals in your database that can help you reach your goals quicker.

There is definitely a right way and a wrong way to do this, so make sure you're educated to take advantage of your financial future. Be sure to never buy into the idea that you need to save tons of dollars before you start to implement this plan in your life. Just start where you can with what you have.

Remember to first know exactly where you are in life to determine ideal timeframes of your season of life and risk tolerance.

Ultimately, your financial priorities and plan of attack can be decided only by you. But having a step-by-step financial plan can help you stay on track when you're tempted to go rogue and freestyle with your financial life. Your goals must be bigger than your vices or wants to achieve the success you seek. It's time to replace "I'll get to it eventually" with "I'm doing it right now." It's time to build the financial house you desire that is built on a solid foundation of W.E.A.L.T.H. instead of straws that blow in the wind.

What keeps you from creating a plan of action and sticking to it?

Don't call it a budget, but rather a Financial Success Plan, as the words you use are important. You must be motivated to achieve your goals and most people, including myself, would rather have financial success than a budget.

14

Harvest

Principle: You can't reap valuable rewards until you plant and nurture valuable seeds.

Journey to Americus

Not too long ago I was invited to travel to Americus, Georgia, to serve as the Keynote Speaker for the Boys & Girls Club of America's annual Steak 'n Stake dinner in that small town about 300 miles south of Atlanta. Because it was close to the end of the summer and the weather was still great, I decided to drive down and I asked my wife, who rarely travels with me, to join me for the trip. I always love to get opportunities to speak in front of crowds, but this opportunity was a little unique, which caused me to be more excited than usual. One of the selling points to get me in the car and on the back roads of Georgia was that my wife and I would have dinner with former United States of America President Jimmy Carter, and then he would be introducing me to deliver my keynote. As if that weren't enough, I was told he was looking forward to meeting me. "How cool was this?" I thought as my wife Jan and I prepared for the trip. After living in Georgia for more than 20 years, I've become accustomed to the beautiful countryside and love to take advantage to take drives in the country especially when the leaves on the trees are at their brightest preparing for season's change.

The landscape was beautifully painted in golds, yellows, reds, and orange, which served as beautifully crafted music to my range of view. I noticed field after field being Harvested and it hit me like never before. The men and women I saw working in the field had worked all year for this moment. It was time to Harvest. They had labored hard all year round, prayed for the rain, and hoped for enough sunshine and not too much wind—basically they wanted the perfect conditions. There had been a lot of planning as well as a lot of waiting. Now was the time to gather all that they had waited and worked so hard for.

What the Harvest Means

It made me stop and really think about what the Harvest meant to these farmers. Growing up in Detroit, I didn't understand the significance of farming until I saw my first farm. I didn't give any thought to what it took to run a farm until I talked to a farmer. The more I began to see how it worked and understood the significance, plus what it took to make it work, I realized it was a lot like our financial lives. Think about all the things you work hard for, as well as the waiting and praying that you will have something to gather a bounty from your hard work.

My mother would talk about the excitement she felt during Harvest time growing up in Arkansas on the farm. She shared stories that described the dust, the busy chores, and her brothers taking turns riding in the combine and on the tractor.

"There was a feeling in the air," she explained.

Remembering that made me think about all of the hard work my grandfather invested in a plot of land. He put his blood, sweat, and tears into the land. He was committed to back-breaking work and overcoming challenges to ensure that he had all he needed to prepare the soil to ensure that it was just right to receive the seeds—similar to the way you must prepare your mind to accomplish a task. Whether it's the task of discovering exactly who you are, which for all intents and purposes you are the farmer. You are the one who identifies the plot of land, determines if it's ripe for planting, and finds what it is that you're passionate about, what comes naturally, and what keeps you engaged. Maybe it's knowing and being honest about your current financial position, which might cause you to put pride aside to ask for help.

It became evident that it was much more than a mere act of doing, but it was also knowing that you didn't toil in vain. It was confirmation that your due diligence and hard work were purposeful. Sure, it might seem difficult to create a plan, cut back on spending, save until it hurts, or work hard to achieve your goals by leveraging your assets, but see yourself as the farmer in the field experiencing that Harvest feeling that permeated the country air.

You might have just experienced a cold season, and therefore your Harvest wasn't very plentiful. The circumstances of life have caused you to stop planting because you haven't experienced the Harvest that you envisioned yet, but that doesn't mean it's time to stop. Instead, it's time to take the wisdom you've established along with the assets you've accumulated along your journey to create a plan that you can use as your leverage to reap your Harvest. When you've worked hard to move forward and manage the resources you've been given or maybe stretching your dollars until they couldn't stretch any further while working your plot of land, you can appreciate a Harvest even more.

What Is Your Harvest?

Even if it is back-breaking work, you must remind yourself that you are working on maximizing your W.E.A.L.T.H. and becoming a better manager of your resources and assets. To ensure that these things manifest themselves, you must realize you are working on building a solid foundation that can become the edifice that you are proud of and provides for many generations to come.

To maximize your opportunity for a great Harvest, you must

- Make sure the conditions are appropriate to plant. Know exactly where and what you are planting. The saying "garbage in, garbage out" also rings true when planting. You must plant quality to reap quality.

- Protect from pests. Keep all things that don't belong in your crops out. It is your job to protect all that you have; therefore, you must make decisions that benefit the crop. Pests in your Harvest might be emergencies or unexpected expenses that pop up and threaten your Harvest.

- Have the right amount of nourishment. You must be sure to give your crops the right amount of tender love and care, attention, time, and planning to make sure that they have the correct balance of nutrients needed to flourish.

- Reduce exposure to unfavorable climates. Your crops were created to grow in a particular environment. If that environment begins to change, you want to be sure that it's ripe for the growth you desire. You might have experienced pain due to financial challenges, setbacks, or shortcomings, but this doesn't mean you have no crops, just that the conditions are not as favorable as they could or should be. So you must work to change them and not allow your crops to die.

Too much rain can cause your crops to become oversaturated and die, but not enough rain can cause your Harvest to shrivel and die before you have the opportunity to reap the rewards. Therefore, it's your job to keep the right mix of knowledge, exposure, resources, and energy vested in your crops to make sure your family will have a Harvest. Their lives will have a bounty that you can't even imagine.

You will have a Harvest because of how you choose to deal with the challenges, by working instead of waiting, planting instead of pouting, and tiling instead of talking. Your Harvest will come from your choices, whether you make choices from scratch or make choices because of the result of someone else's choices. It all results in collected bounty you call your Harvest. As with anything in life, you reap what you sow, so those things that are so important to you must be the things you love most, and take the time to care, work, and fight for. So, this is a great way to look at life and remember that you must be diligent in all that you do and continue to plant the right seeds and pray for rain.

To track and monitor your progress, you must be sure that you have established the six steps that you plan to receive the best Harvest possible.

You Must Have Processes, Plans, and Structures

These components must be in place for managing your financial life and the resources and assets available to you. These processes, plans, and structures must be connected to each other and your life rather than operating separately outside of your plan. To enable plan execution excellence, you must integrate all these processes and structures and align them with your plan. This plan must also be actively managed and improved on an ongoing basis to remain relevant and effective.

Accept the Facts

Many people refuse to face the truth of their situation. You must take full responsibility and ownership for where you are right now. Ignoring the problem makes it worse. You must face the truth and then recognize the lesson that can be learned from that truth. Once you see the lesson, it's time to adapt to your newfound reality and change accordingly. This is essential to successful plan execution and achievement.

Be Accountable

You become a product of your behaviors, beliefs, and values, which is built in all facets of your life. Be dedicated to action and following through. You must define, value, support, and reward yourself for your commitment to accomplishment, which serves as the foundation of accountability for results achievement.

Review Your Plan and Action Steps Daily

You must actively facilitate plan execution. Revisit the fundamentals of your Financial Success Plan to its effectiveness, progress, and potential to facilitate change in your financial life.

Focus on Strengths

To be successful at executing this plan, you must focus on your strengths and delegate the rest. Know what areas you're skilled in and where you are not. You must have the right people with the right skills doing the right job in the right place at the right time.

Make Strategy Execution Personal

When you are invested in something, you naturally commit to making sure that it is sustainable and successful. When you can see the possibilities and begin to see some results, whether small or big, you experience a sense of execution and achievement. You must remain encouraged and realize that your financial success depends on how well your plan is crafted to meet your specific needs and also your ability to execute the plan. Remain committed to making progress with your plan execution while remaining committed to making progress, which helps you remain encouraged and motivated. Your commitment to achieving the results you desire is what will propel you. You must remember the lean times or times when you were without the essentials you needed to live the life you envision. Allow yourself to explore those feelings from the past and use them to serve as your inspiration to press forward. The idea is to do everything within your power to avoid going back to unfavorable situations. Your plan, along with the correct W.E.A.L.T.H. mindset and the steps to execute effectively and efficiently, will get you there.

You must continue to assess and build your current assets and capabilities. Next you can begin to systematically close the gap from where you are to where you want to be. The key is to change your mind and your life will follow.

This journey to Americus made me think about what my Harvest was. This is when it all came full circle. I realized that my Harvest was the manifestation of my "why." It was getting what I needed to supply or fulfill my "why." It was the culmination of a plan implemented and executed with excellence. It was the money I set out to make from my business. It was reaching the savings goal that I thought I would never reach. It was rebuilding my credit when I thought there was no recovery in sight for me. It was my children growing as well as my relationships and business. It was my assets becoming stronger and multiplying to help me reach my goals and fulfill my dreams.

As we reached Americus, it was almost time for me to head over to the college where I would be speaking. When we arrived, I was taken to an area where a VIP reception was held for the donors, honorees, and speakers. As soon as I walked in, there he was. The 39th President of the United States Jimmy Carter with his wife Rosalynn. I was in awe already, but then the former President standing there with secret service in tow told me that he had been looking forward to meeting me. He said that my bio was impressive and he was proud of the work I had been doing to help those in need, something he had dedicated his life to.

President Carter shared stories of being in the Navy, college, helping his father with the peanut farm, and being a plumber for 17 years. He truly knew the meaning of planting and reaping. It just so happened that his Harvest was the highest office in the nation, but in his reality that was just one of many, and in the end his biggest Harvest was where he helped those who needed it most.

At that moment, I realized that my Harvest was manifesting. I was experiencing the fruit of my labor, the rewards for sticking to a plan and not only setting but also achieving goals. I felt like I was in the field, riding the tractor with the aroma of fresh country air filling my senses, realizing the seeds I had sown were now being reaped in this year's Harvest. And not long after, I began to set my sights on the next Harvest.

Remember, you already possess the power and the W.E.A.L.T.H. Now you have to apply it to your life to reap your Harvest.

What do you consider to be your Harvest?

Whatever you plant in the soil of your mind is what will multiply and spring forth.

Remember...

You must also have some practical knowledge and tools at your fingertips to carry out your plan.

Know yourself better than anyone and know what motivates you and discourages you.

Know what you will and won't do to succeed.

Don't be discouraged by where you are now, but rather use it as fuel to propel you.

Set realistic W.E.A.L.T.H. goals that you are committed to carrying out.

Paint the picture of success so clearly you can see it.

Make your "why" so strong that it pushes you to continue even when you want to quit.

Continue to build your non-monetary assets and know how to convert them.

Always use whatever you have to get that which you desire. Remember, you always have something.

Continue to remind yourself that you can have whatever you set your mind on; if you assess your inventory and know how to leverage what you have by creating a plan of action, ultimately you will acquire the wealth you seek by using the W.E.A.L.T.H. you've been given.

Index

P–Q